MONARCH ILLUSTRATED GUIDE TO

BOATING

by Bruce Gossett

MONARCH PRESS

Cover and Text Illustrations by Leonard B. Cole

Published by
MONARCH PRESS, a Simon & Schuster Division of
Gulf & Western Corporation
Simon & Schuster Building
1230 Avenue of the Americas
New York, N.Y. 10020

ISBN: 0-671-18765-1

Manufactured in the United States of America

Table of Contents

One	Types of Powered Boats	7
Two	Boat Terminology	25
Three	Types of Hulls	31
Four	Motors	45
Five	Equipment	55
Six	Insurance and Liability	71
Seven	Fueling	73
Eight	Boat Handling	77
Nine	Boating Laws and Rules of the Road	85
Ten	Piloting and Navigating	91
Eleven	Weather	103
Twelve	In Case of Emergency	109
Thirteen	Maintenance and Upkeep	119
Fourteen	Berthing the Boat	129
Fifteen	Sailing	131
Sixteen	Specialized Craft	161

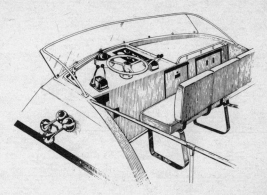

Chapter 1
Types of Powered Boats

Boating is one of the main recreational activities of Americans. It is estimated that over 50 million people participate in the leisure joys of boating. The most popular type of boat, accounting for more than three-quarters of those sold, is the motor or powered boat. One reason for the powered boat's popularity is that, after only brief instruction, the skills necessary for its operation are easily learned. There are many different types of powered boat, each with its own use and personality.

Houseboats

In recent years, the houseboat has become an increasingly popular way of traveling lakes, rivers, and waterways. The houseboat is not manufactured for and should not be used in coastal or open waters.

Livability is the prime concern of the houseboat, and it probably offers more usable space per area and per dollar than any other type of

Houseboat

boat. The usual layout consists of a well-equipped galley in the midships section (where any seesawing motion is least noticeable), a dinette which converts into a double bed, a living room, and an ample head. Usual accommodations include hot and cold running water, showers, front and back porches, and a sundeck. The houseboat ranges in length from 18 to more than 40 feet and even the smallest, an 18-footer, has enough room to sleep four.

The development of the planing hull has simplified houseboat construction and lowered costs. There are no compound curves or jutting frame members to complicate the building and take space away

from the living quarters. Houseboats are usually made of either aluminum or plywood, as they are designed for the more tranquil inland waters. Therefore they avoid the expense of the special, more sturdy materials used in the manufacture of open-sea craft. In addition, due to the size of the living quarters, standard appliances, such as stoves and refrigerators, can be fitted into houseboats, replacing the need for more costly, compact items.

Houseboats can be powered by either inboard or outboard motors, and the largest can attain speeds in excess of 30 MPH.

Hydroplanes

Hydroplanes are designed for racing and fast travel, holding one, sometimes two, occupants. They derive their name from the ability of their hull to skim the surface of the water. Only a minimum amount of hull area is in contact with the water when the boat travels at speed.

Hydroplane

Hydroplanes are specialized sport boats and are fitted with motors powerful enough to plane them. With a 7.5 hp motor they can reach speeds of about 16 MPH; with a 25 hp motor 30 MPH is possible.

Runabouts

Runabouts are open, family sport boats 14 to 20 feet long. They are not suitable for long-distance cruising, since they have neither the size nor the capacity for it. They are, however, suited for speed and fun.

Most runabouts are outboard powered, having motors ranging from 35 to 75 hp, and are constructed of fiberglass or plywood.

Tri-hull Runabout

There are two types of runabouts with different hull designs: the tri-hull and the V-hull. Because it is wider at the bow, the tri-hull is considered the more stylish and has become popular as a family runabout. Its greater width also allows for forward seating and keeping track of the kids. The tri-hull has the ability to cross heavy seas.

V-hull Runabout

The V-hull runabout is more specialized. It presents less surface area to the water, reducing friction, which gives it a faster start than a comparable tri-hull and better handling. V-hull runabouts are more often used as ski and racing boats because of these qualities. Generally, ski boats are fitted with at least a 60 hp motor.

Utility Boats

Utility boats are more commonly, and perhaps more aptly referred to as fishing boats. Their main purpose is to take a man or two out to the fishing area and bring him back.

There are two types of utility boats. The rowing type is a flat-bottomed skiff, 10 to 16 feet long, made of fiberglass, plywood, or wood planking. It looks like a rowboat slightly modified for outboard power.

Utility Boat

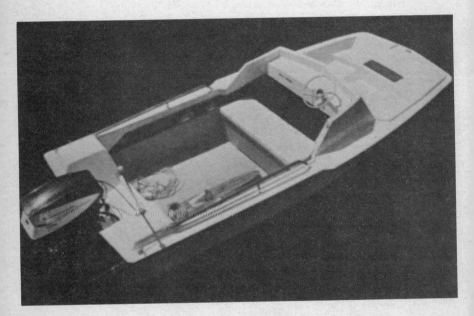

The other kind of utility boat is specially designed to get the most from the outboard motors available. They are the least expensive powered boat on the market and are similar to runabouts though with less comfort and trim. They have a seat for the operator and an electric starter. Adequately powered utility boats can be as fast as runabouts and are not uncommonly used as ski boats.

Very stable due to their large beam, these planing-hull boats can have either a round or a V-bottom. They vary in size from 12 to 24 feet and the motors available range from 7.5 hp for the smaller, lighter ones to 35-, 50-, 75-hp motors to power the 24-footers.

Cruisers

Cruisers are inboard or outboard open-sea craft with an enclosed cabin and cockpit area. They fall within two general classes: the cabin cruiser and the day cruiser.

The cabin cruiser is a weekend or vacation vessel, as it comes equipped with adequate fuel and fresh water facilities to allow for at least two days at sea. It has a fully-enclosed cabin and varies in length from 16 to 25 feet; a 22-footer is considered optimum for the average family. The "sedan" class of cabin cruiser has a minimum of 6 feet headroom throughout; the large cabin area is constructed at the expense of the cockpit area.

Day cruisers are less expensive than cabin cruisers, having a smaller cabin area and lacking overnight facilities. A sleeping area can, however, be improvised by the owner with either sleeping bags or air mattresses. Day cruisers range in size from 15 to 22 feet.

Cruiser

The Sport Fisherman

A recent trend has been to define the sport fisherman as an over 30-foot craft with cruising capabilities.

Sport Fisherman

Though having similar power plants, the cruiser and the sport fisherman differ in design. Since its function is the pursuit and landing of fish, the sport fisherman has most of its useable space devoted to work area, rather than plush cabin surroundings as in a cruiser. Its interiors are usually sparse, consisting of a galley, a head, and a minimal dinette. It has a larger cockpit and smaller cabin area. Also, the sport fisherman, with a lower freeboard than a cruiser, makes it easier to fight and boat a fish since the angler is closer to the waterline. There is a fish-well at the stern for holding the catch.

Motor Yacht

Motor Yachts

Motor yachts are at least 50 feet long and are capable of lengthy cruises because of large water and fuel tanks. They differ from cruisers in cabin layout. A motor yacht has a cabin in the stern, whereas in a cruiser, an aft cockpit lies within the freeboard.

A motor yacht can be powered by two separate engines, each driving its own propeller, or, in the case of the larger ones, by a diesel engine. A large percentage of motor yachts have hulls constructed of wood.

Motor yachts are not lightly referred to as floating mansions. Usual accommodations include a deckhouse, two or more staterooms, a salon, and quarters for the help.

INTERNATIONAL ALPHABET FLAGS, PHONETIC ALPHABET, MORSE CODE AND SEMAPHORE ALPHABET

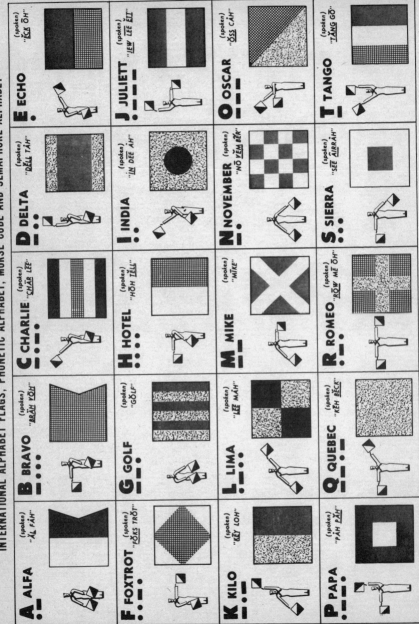

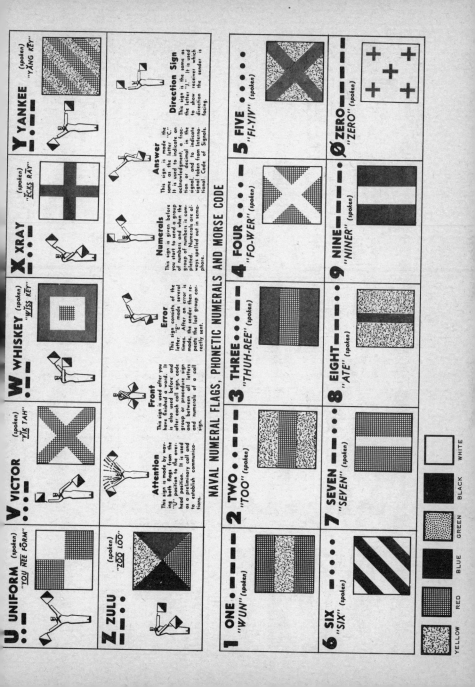

U UNIFORM (spoken) "YOU NEE FORM"
V VICTOR (spoken) "VIK TAH"
W WHISKEY (spoken) "WISS KEY"
X XRAY (spoken) "ECKS RAY"
Y YANKEE (spoken) "YANG KEY"
Z ZULU (spoken) "ZOO LOO"

Attention
This sign is made by waving both flags from the "U" position to the overhead position. It is used as a preliminary call to establish communications.

Front
This sign is used after you have finished a word. It is also used before and after each call sign, code groups and between letters and numerals of a call sign.

Error
This sign consists of the letter "E" mode several times. After an error is made, the sender then repeats the last group correctly sent.

Numerals
This sign is given before you start to send a group of numbers and when the group of numbers is completed. Numerals are always spelled out in semaphore.

Answer
This sign is made the same as the letter "C". It is used to indicate reception of a signal, and to indicate acknowledgment, a fraction or decimal in the signal, and to indicate a signal token from International Code of Signals.

Direction Sign
This sign is the same as the letter "J". It is used to show the receiver which direction the sender is facing.

NAVAL NUMERAL FLAGS, PHONETIC NUMERALS AND MORSE CODE

1 ONE •———— "W'UN" (spoken)
2 TWO ••——— "TOO" (spoken)
3 THREE •••—— "THUH-REE" (spoken)
4 FOUR ••••— "FO-WER" (spoken)
5 FIVE ••••• "FI-YIV" (spoken)
6 SIX —•••• "SIX" (spoken)
7 SEVEN ——••• "SEVEN" (spoken)
8 EIGHT ———•• "ATE" (spoken)
9 NINE ————• "NINER" (spoken)
Ø ZERO ————— "ZERO" (spoken)

YELLOW   RED   BLUE   GREEN   BLACK   WHITE

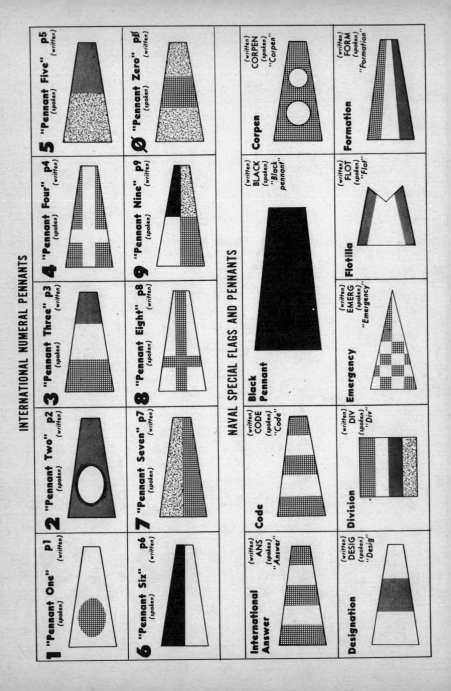

INTERNATIONAL NUMERAL PENNANTS

1 "Pennant One" (spoken) P1 (written)

2 "Pennant Two" (spoken) p2 (written)

3 "Pennant Three" (spoken) p3 (written)

4 "Pennant Four" (spoken) p4 (written)

5 "Pennant Five" (spoken) p5 (written)

6 "Pennant Six" (spoken) p6 (written)

7 "Pennant Seven" (spoken) p7 (written)

8 "Pennant Eight" (spoken) p8 (written)

9 "Pennant Nine" (spoken) p9 (written)

Ø "Pennant Zero" (spoken) pØ (written)

NAVAL SPECIAL FLAGS AND PENNANTS

International Answer (written) ANS (spoken) "Answer"

Code (written) CODE (spoken) "Code"

Black Pennant (written) BLACK (spoken) "Black pennant"

Corpen (written) CORPEN (spoken) "Corpen"

Designation (written) DESIG (spoken) "Desig"

Division (written) DIV (spoken) "Div"

Emergency (written) EMERG (spoken) "Emergency"

Flotilla (written) FLOT (spoken) "Flot"

Formation (written) FORM (spoken) "Formation"

NAVAL SPECIAL FLAGS AND PENNANTS

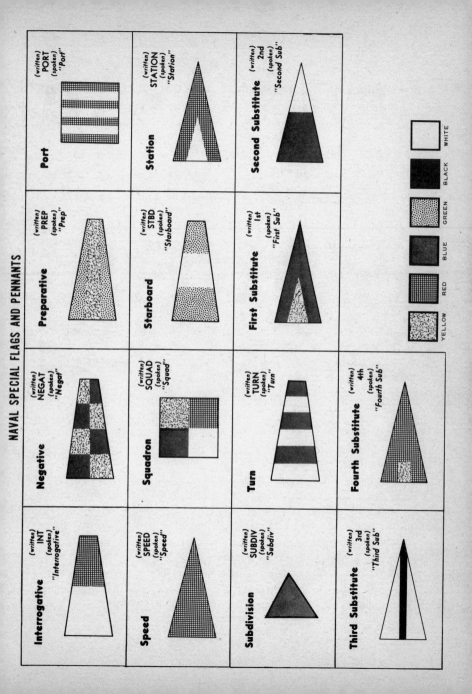

Motor Sailers

Motor sailers, as their name implies, are a marriage of motor and sail boat. Most motor sailers lean toward one or the other means of travel; either they are more motor and less sail, or more sail and less motor.

When used primarily as motorboats, the sail functions to conserve fuel and to steady the boat in wind. As primarily sail, the motor contributes to easier moorings, helps steady the course, and provides an extra push when speed is desired.

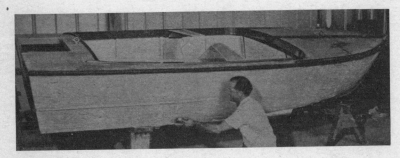

Kit Boat

Do-It-Yourself Boats

Do-it-yourself boat kits are available from most of the leading boat builders. The kits come with complete step-by-step instructions.

There are a variety of options possible. A do-it-yourselfer can buy only the plans for a few dollars and purchase the materials from his local supplier, or he can buy just the hull and put everything else together himself, or a complete kit can be purchased and assembled with just the use of ordinary hand tools.

Since the biggest cost of a new boat is labor, a saving of 50 to 65 percent is possible. Working nights and weekends, a kit boat, depending on its complexity, can be assembled in better than six weeks.

Hydrofoils

Hydrofoils were first experimented with in this country by Alexander Graham Bell. They have thin foils placed at both sides of the hull. When the boat reaches planing speed, the hull lifts completely out of the water and rests on the foil members. Because the hull is a few feet above the waterline, the passengers have a very dry ride. In addition, the boat is able to weather rough water fairly successfully, as only the small surface of the foils is exposed to the motion of the waves.

Hydrofoils have been used experimentally in New York City as commuter boats.

Hydrofoil

Chapter 2
Boat Terminology

Each year more and more Americans buy their first boat and begin to realize the special feeling of freedom that ownership brings. But there is more to boating than buying a boat. There is the history and the tradition, and part of the tradition is the language. Though technology has vastly altered the face of boating in the past few decades, the terminology has remained largely unchanged. Learning the language of boating is one way of contact with its colorful past.

There is a practical aspect as well. Boat terminology is concise and its meaning is instantly communicated. Suppose you and your family are mooring a boat, and your wife yells, "Watch out for the left edge!" If she happens to be facing in a different direction than you, you may very well turn into the dock. For example, port is always to the left when you face the bow, or front of the boat. If it is said that something is off the port, you know it is on the left.

The following simplified boat diagrams and 100-word glossary are not meant to turn you into an old salt. They will provide you with a basis for understanding your boat and, perhaps, increase your enjoyment.

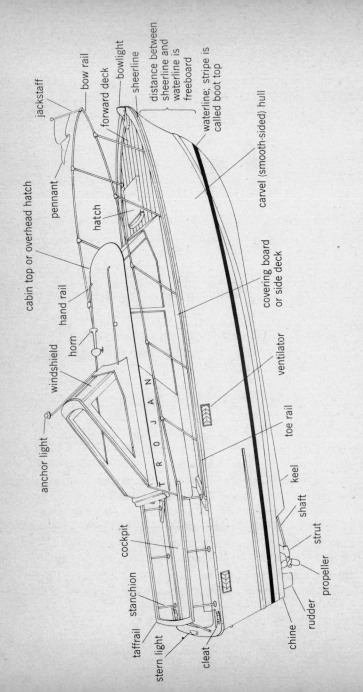

The parts of a motorboat. (*Courtesy Trojan Boat Company.*)

Simplified Boat Diagram

GLOSSARY

Abeam—alongside, abreast of the boat
Aft—at or near the rear of the boat
Amidships—middle of the boat; halfway between the front and the rear
Astern—behind the boat
Athwartships—from side to side of the boat; opposite of fore-and-aft
Bail—to throw water from a boat
Barnacle—form of salt-water marine life which grows on ship bottoms
Beam—greatest width of a boat
Below—under the deck
Berth—mooring place for a boat
Bilge—bottom of the hull
Bilge pump—a device to pump water from the hull
Binnacle—compass cover
Block—pully
Boat hook—a pole with a metal hook; used for retrieving objects from
       the water or for handling small boats alongside the dock
Bollards—short heavy beams on a pier, used for tying up boats
Boot top—thin strip of paint at the water line
Bow—front end of the boat
Broadside—entire side of the boat
Bulkhead—boat wall
Car-topper—boat able to be carried atop a car
Cat-walk—deck alongside the cabin
Cavitation—occurs when air is pulled from the surface to around the
       propeller; causes loss of power
Ceiling—lining of thin planks inside the rib
Chart—marine road map
Chine—lowest edge of the hull where sides and bottom join
Chock—horizontal eyelet affixed to the deck; used as a guide for lines
Cleat-small T-like projections from the deck used to secure lines
Coaming—cockpit sides above the deck line
Cockpit—the helm; also open deck sections for passengers
Companionway—steps leading below from the deck

Cradle—wooden framework used for onshore boat support

Cuddy—small cabin under fore-deck of a runabout

Deck—floor of the boat

Displacement—weight of the boat, measured as the total amount of water displaced by the hull

Draft—depth of the hull from waterline to keel

Ebb tide—outgoing tide

Eddy—circular swirl of water

Even keel—properly trimmed

Fast—secured

Fathom—six feet of water depth

Fenders—cushions along the outside of the boat

Flood tide—incoming tide

Flybridge—cockpit mounted above the regular cockpit; used for better visibility and deep-sea fishing.

Following sea—waves approaching from the rear of the boat

Fore—front of the boat (bow)

Fore-and-aft—lengthwise; opposite of athwartships

Freeboard—length of the boat sides above the waterline

Galley—kitchen

Grab rails—hand holds

Grapnel—small, hooked anchor

Gunwale—topmost rail or side

Hatch—deck opening

Head—toilet

Helm—pilot's control station; also the steering machinery, including rudder and wheel

Hitch—easily loosened knot

Hold—interior of the boat

Hull—shell of the boat

Inboard—within or part of the hull

Keel—runs along the bottom center of the hull; backbone of the boat

Knot—measure of water speed; equal to one nautical mile per hour

Lee—area sheltered from the wind

Leeward—direction away from the wind

Line—boat rope

List—slant of a boat to one side

Lurch—sudden rolling

Marina—boat basin

Midships—broadest part of a ship

Moor—secure a boat

Nautical mile—equal to 6,080 feet or one minute of latitude

Outboard—attached to or outside the hull

Painter—mooring line of a small boat

Pitch—fore-and-aft motion

Planing—skimming the surface of the water

Port—left side of the boat, looking toward the bow

Quarter—either side of the boat at the aft

Rib—hull frame member

Rode—anchor line or cable

Roll—sideways motion

Rudder—vertical fin attached to the hull behind the propeller; turns the boat by pushing the stern sideways

Running lights—nighttime navigation lights

Screw—propeller

Scupper—hole allowing water to run off the deck

Sea anchor—cone-shaped device trailed from the stern to keep the boat heading into the wind

Sheer—the top edge of the deck or rail

Skeg—stabilizing fin usually supporting the rudder

Starboard—right side of the boat, facing the bow

Stern—rear end of the boat

Superstructure—all the structure above the deck

Tiller—steering handle attached to the outboard motor (or rudder)

Topside—above the waterline

Transom—back of boat across the stern from which the outboard motor is hung

Trim—manner of floating according to arrangement of weight and/or sail

Trough—cavity between two waves

Underbody—hull below the waterline
Wake—track of waves and foam left astern of a moving boat
Waterline—line at which the water meets the hull
Weather—direction from which the wind blows
Windward—toward the wind; same as weather
Yaw—swing of an off-course boat

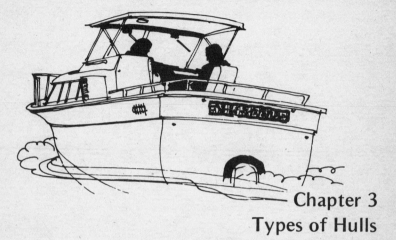

Chapter 3
Types of Hulls

There are really only two different types of hulls, the displacement hull and the planing hull. All other types are modifications of one or a combination of both.

Displacement Hulls

Displacement hulls are so named because, as they travel, they displace, or dislodge, their own weight of water. The weight of a displacement-hull boat is calculated on this basis. For example, a 12,000-ton boat does not weight 12,000 tons if you were to lift it from the water and place it on a scale. Its hull will displace 12,000 tons of water as it moves.

In theory, a displacement hull cannot go faster than the square root of its waterline multiplied by 1½. This means that a boat with a 25-foot waterline has a maximum speed of 7½ MPH. (The square root of 25 is five; five times 1½ yields 7½.) As much power as can be bought can be put behind such a boat, but its speed will never be much greater than 7½ MPH. On the other hand, if the boat were heavily laden with cargo and had the same power, it would not travel appreciably slower than 7½ MPH. This is because the added weight will lower the boat in the water, increasing the waterline. This in turn will increase the displacement and compensate for the additional weight.

Displacement-hull Boat

A displacement hull slices through the water. Small surface waves have little effect on its performance, as the main bulk of the hull is below the wave. In heavy seas, a displacement-hull boat can travel at almost full speed. It is easier to hold on course and handle in winds than any other type of hull design.

The long deep keel of a displacement-hull boat, besides improving its stability, also allows for a more ample cabin below decks. The displacement hull is a popular design for cruisers or any other type of boat where space is a prime concern.

Planing-hull Boat

Planing Hulls

A planing hull skims the surface of the water. It is capable of great speed since it is not limited by a large surface area in contact with the water, as a displacement hull. The more power supplied the faster the boat will travel. The only limits are air friction and the friction of the surface water.

Boats fitted with planing hulls must reach the planing-hull speed before they can begin to skim the water. The planing-hull speed is roughly more than 15 MPH. Until it reaches planing speed it is a displacement hull. Operating at less than planing speed it is hard to handle. This is because a planing hull is lighter and comparatively flatter than a displacement hull.

Because a pure planing hull rides the surface just about every wave transmits a shock through the boat. In rough weather this can be a great disadvantage. It has to be slowed down or the waves may literally shake the boat to pieces. And if one happens to slow to below planing speed, the boat becomes hard to control.

This inability to handle choppy, open seas has resulted in modifications of the pure planing hull. One such design, employed in runabouts, combines a displacement-type V-hull with the planing hull. The actual planing surface is shifted toward the aft, with the V-hull forward. This results in a boat easier to handle on open water, though there is some sacrifice of planing speed.

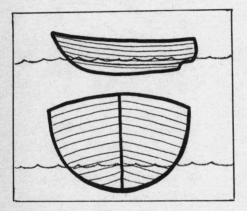

Diagram of Round Bottom

Round Bottom

Round-bottom hulls are eminently seaworthy displacement hulls. They are probably the oldest of the hull designs. Because they are curved, round-bottom hulls are not easily constructed and, hence, are expensive.

The rounded bottom makes for a comfortable ride. Fitted onto many low-speed fishing boats, it is easily propelled because it meets little water resistance. A round-bottom hull is also quite strong and is preferable for rough-water cruising boats and sailers.

Flat Bottom

A flat-bottom displacement hull is the easiest and most inexpensive hull to build. It makes for an exceptionally stable craft able to transport heavy loads.

The usual criticism of a flat bottom is that it is unseaworthy. It tends toward pounding more than any other hull type. However, there are flat-bottom boats, such as certain dory modifications and garveys, which have little trouble in open water. Generally, ignoring these exceptions, a flat bottom is a shallow-water craft suitable only in protected inland waters. It is used on small rowboats and fishing outboards.

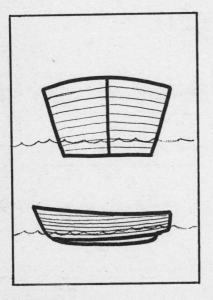

Flat Bottom

Tri-hull

A tri-hull has, compared to a V-hull, a flat bow. This opens up the interior space for additional seating and storage. It is heavier than a V-hull, offering a larger surface to the water. A tri-hull makes for an extremely stable boat, and the extra bow space can be used as a diving platform.

A tri-hull is slower than a comparable V-hull in reaching planing speed. Because of the complex curves of the design, tri-hulls are constructed of molded fiberglass. They are popularly used on family-style runabouts.

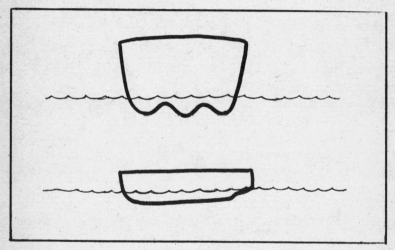

Tri-hull

Tunnel Drive

TUNNEL DRIVE

A tunnel drive is an ordinary deep V-hull modified by a hydrodynamic tunnel above the keel line. The propeller shaft is placed within the tunnel, resulting in better performance and greater speed without the use of a larger motor.

In most conventional inboards the shaft is at an angle and the propeller drives a good deal of the water downward. In a tunnel-drive boat the propelled water is driven horizontally. An added push is achieved by the tunnel. As the boat moves a vacuum is created within the tunnel which the water, with considerable force, rushes in to fill, thereby forcing a greater amount of water into the propeller.

A tunnel-drive hull results in improved forward steering, due to the rush of water against the rudder, and quick turning even at slow speeds. Developed only a few years ago, tunnel drives have been used on runabouts.

Hull Materials

Wood

Wood hulls have natural sound-absorbing qualities and provide insulation against vibrations. They combine light weight and strength. It is easier to build a wood hull than any other type, because wood is simply worked, requiring only hand tools. However, given all of this, wood hulls are found mainly on extremely expensive boats (over $50,000) or on very cheap ones.

This apparent contradiction is due to wood's main disadvantage: upkeep. Wood hulls are subject to all sorts of maladies. Resting out of the water during the off-season they can succumb to dry rot. Afloat they are easy targets for shipworms, such as marine borers and teredos. They must be periodically sanded and painted to protect the hull from infestations.

Wood Hull Boat

Also, after a season out of the water, wood hulls will leak from one to seven days as the shrunken dry boards swell to their watertight position.

Wood Hull Boat—Lapstrake

There are a variety of woods used in hull construction. The better grades of cedar, cypress, and heavy yellow pine are rot resistant. Lignum vitae is worm resistant and very heavy. Teak is resistant to both rot and shipworms, but very rare and expensive. Oak is easy to work with, but prone to rot. Wood hulls made of plywood are heavy and the lamination can come apart under repeated swelling and shrinking.

There are two types of wood hulls. In a caravel hull the planks are laid flat, side-by-side, giving the hull a smooth appearance. The seams often crack when they dry and most need fresh caulking every season.

The lapstrake hull avoids the necessity of caulking. In a lapstrake, each horizontal plank overlaps the plank directly beneath it. It is slower than a comparable caravel, because its larger surface area results in greater water friction. Also, a lapstrake is more trouble to sand and paint.

Aluminum

Aluminum is used in the manufacture of small, lightweight, inexpensive boats, such as utility car-toppers. Because of salt-water electrolysis, an aluminum boat not constructed of special marine-grade aluminum will decompose after about one week. Electrolysis can be a serious problem for most metal boats. Sea water contains metallic salts which, under the current caused by an improperly grounded motor, can replace or corrode the metal in a hull.

Aluminum-hull Boat

Most aluminum car-toppers are fitted with a flotation device which will prevent the boat from sinking even if capsized.

The lightness of this malleable metal allows it to be easily molded into pleasing shapes, as in a small runabout. However, once afloat the lightness can be a serious disadvantage. At runabout speeds, the bow tends to rise, and a wind getting beneath the hull can make for difficult steering.

Steel

Steel hulls are not generally used any longer in boat manufacturing. As with other metallic hulls, steel hulls are subject to noise and vibration and must be sprayed on the inside with a sound-deadening material.

Steel hulls are extremely strong and able to take severe wave pounding. However, they make for heavy boats difficult to drydock. The main drawback of a steel hull is that it must be constantly maintained to prevent rust.

Fiberglass

Fiberglass is one of the most durable and strongest of the hull materials used. It requires only minimal maintenance, as it is immune to shipworms and rot.

The one-piece hull has no seams and therefore no leaks. If punctured it can be easily repaired and, if scratched, it need not be

Fiberglass Boat

retouched because most fiberglass hulls are color impregnated. Also, a fiberglass hull needs few frame members, uncluttering the inside space and allowing for a roomier belowdecks.

Fiberglass weighs less than wood, but it is still quite heavy. Unlike wood, however, fiberglass does not naturally float and the hull should be fitted with flotation devices. Fiberglass is used in runabouts, motor yachts, and houseboats.

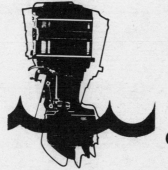

Chapter 4
Motors

Choosing the right motor for your boat can often be confusing. If too small a motor is installed, it will be overworked, subject to frequent repair, and have a short life. A larger engine than necessary, besides being a waste of money, can overtax the hull, making the boat go faster than it was designed for. It is no easy matter to correctly mesh boat and motor. A reputable dealer is probably the best authority but, before approaching him, you should be aware of at least the basics.

OUTBOARDS

Outboard motors were originally developed for small boats. They were designed as portable low-cost motors to obviate the necessity of rowing. They have since grown up and now outboards can be purchased with 200 hp.

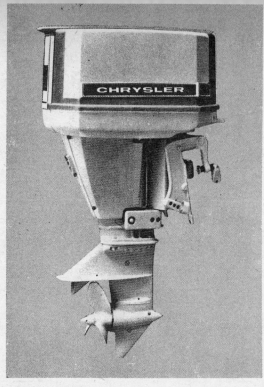

Outboard Motor

Outboards are almost exclusively two-cycle water-cooled engines. The oil mixes directly in the cylinder with the gasoline. When the gasoline is burned away, providing the power, the oil remains to lubricate the cylinder and the moving parts. For a rough estimation of fuel consumption divide the horsepower of the engine by 10. The answer is approximately the number of gallons of gasoline the boat will use in one hour at full throttle.

Outboards account for almost half of all motor boats sold. There are one-cylinder models which can supply 7.5 hp. Two-cylinder outboards are not as noisy as one-cylinder outboards, and can come with up to 55 hp. Three-cylinders usually range from 60 to 85 hp. An optional electric starter is available.

When used on small utility boats, outboards tend to put weight on the stern, limiting performance. However, its advantages on this type of boat far outweigh a decrease in performance. The boat can be easily and exactly steered by the helmsman, since the entire motor is turned in the desired direction. In addition, the motor can be tilted upwards in shallow water and the boat can be beached without propeller damage. Outboards can be removed from the boat to prevent theft.

Outboards are also fitted onto small runabouts and cabin cruisers under 18 feet. A 25-hp outboard provides enough force to propel a 14-foot runabout at 30 MPH. Easy maintenance is possible as an outboard presents its motor openly.

One problem inherent in other types of motors is not applicable to outboards. Gasoline leaks and fumes are removed by the water and atmosphere; they are not able to collect to cause fire or explosion.

The following table is meant to be a guide of outboard power in relation to boat size. It must be emphasized that horsepower depends on a variety of factors, such as hull design and the weight to be propelled.

Overall Boat Length x Transom Width	Maximum Safe Horsepower
30'	2
40'	5
50'	15
60'	30
70'	45
80'	65
90'	80
100'	90
110'	95
120'	100
130'	105
140'	109
150'	111

Inboard

INBOARDS

An inboard boat, unlike an outboard, has a permanently fixed propeller and rudder, which limits the water depth at which it can travel. In shallows, the propeller may be damaged if it comes in contact with the bottom.

Inboards have virtually no limitations to their power. They range from one-cylinder 2-hp motors to eight-cylinder engines capable of 600 hp. They draw upon the surrounding water for cooling, not usually having a self-contained system as in automobiles. Because they are inserted into the body of the boat, inboards should be fitted with bilge blowers to prevent an accumulation of gas fumes.

The standard inboard has three gears; forward, neutral, and reverse (used for breaking). It can come with a reduction gear, which allows a smaller, lighter motor to turn a large propeller. This may be a factor to consider in purchasing, as a large, expensive, powerful engine can have three times the weight and take up three times the space of a small engine. Assume that while cruising, the desired propeller speed is 1500 rpm. A small lightweight 3000 rpm motor fitted with a 2:1 reduction gear will turn the propeller at the desired 1500 rpm, operating at full power. Without the reduction gear, the 3000-rpm motor would turn a smaller propeller and not move the boat as efficiently. In a 26-footer the average reduction gear fitted is 1.5:1. Larger and heavier boats would require a larger reduction gear.

There are three types of inboards. The most expensive is the heavy duty type fitted into large cruisers and houseboats. For average size cruisers, a medium-duty motor should suffice. Runabouts are fitted with high-speed inboards.

The following table is presented as a guide to the relationship of inboard power and boat size. It is only an approximate compilation, as horsepower depends upon hull design and the weight to be pulled.

Overall Boat Length x Transom Width	Maximum Safe Horsepower
30'	4
40'	7
50'	15
60'	30
70'	50
80'	70
90'	90
100	110
110	130
120	150
130	170
140	190

STERNDRIVES (I.O.)

Sterndrives or I.O.'s (inboard outdrives) are a cross between inboard and outboard motors. Like inboards, they are powerful, reliable, and economical. The outdrive can be tilted as on outboards.

Sterndrive Boat

A sterndrive boat is sold as a complete package; the manufacturer blends the boat and motor for the buyer. An outboard, though cheaper, is bought separate from the basic boat. Because boat and motor are matched, good weight distribution is acheived.

Most sterndrives range from 150 to 200 hp. It is an attractive package to the buyer of a 20 to 28 foot boat. Buyers of medium size boats, 15 to 20-footers, have to choose between a sterndrive and an outboard. If the boat is to be used for pleasure and high-speed cruising, then the more economical sterndrive is the better buy. If fishing is to be the main purpose of the boat, then lower fuel costs are not a factor, since much of the running will be at slow speeds.

Easy repair and maintenance is possible on the outdrive. It is detachable from the inboard unit and can be taken to the repair shop. The inboard portion, however, is attached to the boat and must be serviced at dockside.

Jet Engine Boat

JET ENGINES

Boats equipped with a jet engine are propelled by a stream of water forced outward from the stern. Of course, this is the way all powered boats move. But in a jet engine there is no exposed propeller. It is located instead in the turbine-like housing of the motor.

Not having a propeller to worry about, skiers and divers can safely board the boat from the stern. Jet engines are built with 155 to 450 hp.

Diesel Powered Boat

DIESELS

Diesel engines have fewer moving parts than a gasoline engine and operate on lower-priced fuel. A diesel engine does not need spark plugs to ignite the fuel or a carburetor. Air is compressed in the cylinders, heating it, and when the fuel is inserted, it vaporizes and ignites instantly.

Although the diesel is the stronger engine, it is heavier, and hence more costly, than its gasoline counterpart. Only if the boat is used long and frequently will the diesel's fuel saving surmount its high initial cost. For this reason, it is most appropriate for commercial fishing boats and motor yachts.

PROPELLERS

Unlike the tables for outboard and inboard motors presented previously as guides for matching boat length and maximum horse-power, there is no way to gauge the correct propeller for your boat and motor. The efficiency of a propeller depends upon the hull shape and the weight the boat is to carry, as well as the motor driving it. Dissimilar hulls having a similar motor and propeller can have widely different performances.

Without the use of reduction gears, a large motor would take a larger propeller than a smaller motor. The basis of engine power and hence propeller thrust is the rpm. A large motor builds up more force, or torque, per rpm than a small motor. It is therefore better able to turn a heavier, larger propeller against the natural water resistance.

Propellers can be right- or left-handed, rotate clockwise or counterclockwise when viewed from astern. Most marine propellers are right-handed. It is best for maneuvering that the top of the blades curl outward.

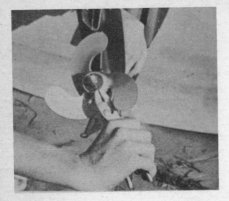
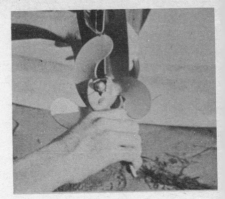

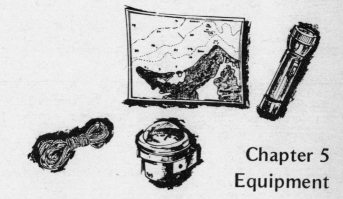

Chapter 5
Equipment

EQUIPMENT REQUIRED BY LAW

The United States Coast Guard has established minimum equipment requirements for all motorboats plying navigable waters. All navigable waters and all coastal waters are under the jurisdiction of the federal government and subject to its regulations. In addition, a state may have its own regulations, but these can in no way diminish or conflict with the federal standards.

The minimum equipment required by federal law varies with the length of the motorboat. The length is measured by a level line running from bow to stern parallel to the centerline. The federal government divides boats into four classes. They are:

Class A: less than 16 feet
Class 1: 16 feet to less than 26 feet
Class 2: 26 feet to less than 40 feet
Class 3: 40 feet to not more than 65 feet.

On the next page are the detailed federal minimum equipment requirements. The table is taken from the Coast Guard booklet CG 290, called *Pleasure Craft: Federal Requirements for Motorboats.* The pamphlet may be gotten from a local Coast Guard Station or from the Government Printing Office by writing the Superintendent of Documents, Washington, D.C. 20402.

NECESSARY EQUIPMENT

Coast Guard regulations detail the bare minimum of equipment necessary for a boat. For safety's sake, the following equipment is deemed necessary and should be purchased. Some items are needed in the everyday, routine running of your boat. Others will not be necessary until an emergency arises, and then it may well be too late to run to the boating store.

Tool Kit

The basic tool kit should include an adjustable end wrench (crescent), slip joint pliers, a pipe wrench, a vise grip, various size screwdrivers, a box and wrench set, and a hammer. Also present in the tool kit should be a couple of spare spark plugs and, perhaps, some replacement engine parts, including a set of distributor points, a condenser, a coil, a fuel pump, and a spare fuel filter.

For marine use, specially manufactured tools of beryllium copper are available. The tools are spark and corrosion resistant, and nonmagnetic. Tools of beryllium copper are considerably more expensive than the usual type.

Rope

There are three kinds of rope that may be purchased. The most

EQUIPMENT REQUIREMENTS

Minimum Required Equipment

EQUIPMENT	CLASS A (Less than 16 feet)	CLASS 1 (16 feet to less than 26 feet)	CLASS 2 (26 feet to less than 40 feet)	CLASS 3 (40 feet to not more than 65 feet)
BACK-FIRE FLAME ARRESTOR	One approved device on each carburetor of all gasoline engines installed after April 25, 1940, except outboard motors.			
VENTILATION	At least two ventilator ducts fitted with cowls or their equivalent for the purpose of properly and efficiently ventilating the bilges of every engine and fuel-tank compartment of boats constructed or decked over after April 25, 1940, using gasoline or other fuel of a flashpoint less than 110° F.			
BELL	None.*	None.*	One, which when struck, produces a clear, bell-like tone of full round characteristics.	
LIFESAVING DEVICES	One approved life preserver, buoyant vest, ring buoy, special purpose water safety buoyant device, or buoyant cushion for each person on board or being towed on water skis, etc.		One approved life preserver or ring buoy for each person on board.	
WHISTLE	None.*	One hand, mouth, or power operated, audible at least ½ mile.	One hand or power operated, audible at least 1 mile.	One power operated, audible at least 1 mile.
FIRE EXTINGUISHER— PORTABLE When NO fixed fire extinguishing system is installed in machinery space(s).	At least One B–1 type approved hand portable fire extinguisher. (Not required on outboard motorboat less than 26 feet in length and not carrying passengers for hire if the construction of such motorboats will not permit the entrapment of explosive or flammable gases or vapors.)		At least Two B–1 type approved hand portable fire extinguishers; OR At least One B–11 type approved hand portable fire extinguisher.	At least Three B–1 type approved hand portable fire extinguishers; OR At least One B–1 type Plus One B–11 type approved hand portable fire extinguisher.
When fixed fire extinguishing system is installed in machinery space(s).	None.	None.	At least One B–1 type approved hand portable fire extinguisher.	At least Two B–1 type approved hand portable fire extinguishers; OR At least One B–11 type approved hand portable fire extinguisher.

Fire extinguishers manufactured after 1 January 1965 will be marked, "Marine Type USCG Type ——— Size ——— Approval No. 162–028. . . ."

*NOTE.—Not required by the Motorboat Act of 1940; however, the "Rules of the Road" require these vessels to sound proper signals.
**NOTE.—Toxic vaporizing-liquid type fire extinguishers, such as those containing carbon tetrachloride or chlorobromomethane, are not accepted as required approved extinguishers on uninspected vessels (private pleasure craft).

Coast Guard Equipment Requirements

widely used is Manila rope. It is low cost, long wearing, but not very strong. Polypropylene rope has about 50 percent more tensile strength than Manila. It floats and is stronger wet than dry. It will not rot or mildew. Polypropylene is used for mooring and towing lines. Nylon is twice as strong, and about twice as expensive as Manila. Being elastic, it is suitable for anchor and mooring lines.

Anchor

An anchor is essential if you want to stop the boat elsewhere than at a dock. Probably the most reliable motorboat anchor is one of the patent types, such as a Danforth or a Northill. They are light and foldable. An 8-pound anchor is recommended for boats up to 16 feet, for 16- to 20-footers a 13-pound anchor should be used, and for craft 20 to 40 feet long, a 22-pounder is suitable.

First-Aid Kit and Manual

Many pre-packaged first-aid kits are inadequate. The most complete kit possible should be bought, and ask your family doctor if there is anything that might be added to the basic kit. The kit should be stored in a watertight container and kept well out of the reach of children. One of the best and most comprehensive manuals is published by the American Red Cross. It is titled *First Aid Textbook* and is available for a small charge from any local chapter.

Auxiliary Power

For use in small boats a telescoping oar, or paddle, can be purchased at little cost. Because the oar is in sections, it is easily stored. Boats equipped with twin motors can limp back to port should one fail. Carrying a spare motor is a needless expense, as the extra weight and space it would occupy makes it unsuitable for any but the largest craft. A spare motor should not be a substitute for proper or careful maintenance of the original.

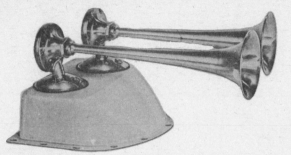

Boat Horn

Horn and Whistle

Under federal law, boats under 16 feet (Class A) are not required to have a horn or whistle. Craft measuring 16 to 26 feet (Class 1) are required to have a horn or whistle audible to one-half mile. Classes 2 and 3 boats, 26 to not more than 65 feet, must carry a horn audible for at least one mile.

However, even if you have a smaller than 16-foot boat, a horn is considered necessary. Rules-of-the-road (see Chapter 9) have precedence over federal law. For example, an overtaking boat should give one blast of its horn or whistle if it intends to pass on the starboard side, and two if it will pass on the portside.

Lights

By federal law, lights are required on all boats underway from sunset to sunrise. A boat is underway if it is not at anchor, not docked, and not aground. If the boat is outside federal waterways, then the boat

Lights Required on Motorboats Under Way Between Sunset and Sunrise

The required lights are listed below. The term "point" is a nautical one (compasses used to be read in "points") and is a little over 11°, thus a 32-point light is visible through an arc of 360°. A 10-point light is visible through an arc of about 110°.

Inland Rules—These lights may be shown only on Inland Waters, Western Rivers, and Great Lakes.[1]

International Rules—Lights under International Rules may be shown on Inland Waters, Western Rivers, and Great Lakes, and are required on the high seas.

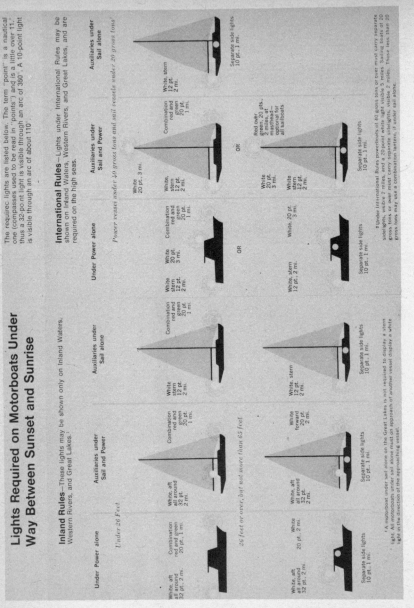

Inland Rules

Under Power alone

Under 26 Feet

White, aft all around 32 pt., 2 mi.
Combination red and green 20 pt., 1 mi.
Separate side lights 10 pt., 1 mi.

26 feet or over, but not more than 65 feet

White, aft all around 32 pt., 2 mi.
White 20 pt., 2 mi.
Separate side lights 10 pt., 1 mi.

Auxiliaries under Sail and Power

White, aft all around 32 pt., 2 mi.
Combination red and green 20 pt., 1 mi.
Separate side lights 10 pt., 1 mi.

White, aft all around 32 pt., 2 mi.
White forward 20 pt., 2 mi.
Separate side lights 10 pt., 1 mi.

Auxiliaries under Sail alone

White stern 12 pt., 2 mi.
Combination red and green 20 pt., 1 mi.
Separate side lights 10 pt., 1 mi.

White stern 12 pt., 2 mi.
Separate side lights 10 pt., 1 mi.

International Rules

Power vessel under 40 gross tons and sail vessels under 20 gross tons[2]

Under Power alone

White 20 pt., 3 mi.
White stern 12 pt., 2 mi.
Combination red and green 20 pt., 1 mi.
Separate side lights 10 pt., 1 mi.

OR

White, stern 12 pt., 2 mi.
White, 20 pt., 3 mi.
Separate side lights 10 pt., 1 mi.

Auxiliaries under Sail and Power

White 20 pt., 3 mi.
White, stern 12 pt., 2 mi.
Combination red and green 20 pt., 1 mi.
Separate side lights 10 pt., 1 mi.

OR

White 20 pt., 3 mi.
White stern 12 pt., 2 mi.
Red over green, 20 pts., 2 miles, at masthead—optional for all sailboats
Separate side lights 10 pt., 1 mi.

Auxiliaries under Sail alone

White, stern 12 pt., 2 mi.
Combination red and green 20 pt., 1 mi.
Separate side lights 10 pt., 1 mi.

[1] A motorboat under sail alone on the Great Lakes is not required to display a stern light. All motorboats under sail alone must on approach of another vessel display a white light in the direction of the approaching vessel.

[2] Under International Rules powerboats of 40 gross tons or over must carry separate sidelights, visible 2 miles, and a 20-point white light visible 5 miles. Sailing boats of 20 gross tons or over must carry separate sidelights, visible 2 miles. Those less than 20 gross tons may use a combination lantern, if under sail alone.

may be lighted according to International Rules, which apply on the open sea. States may have their own set of lighting rules. These may be less rigid, and the federal standards being the stricter would certainly apply.

The angle of light is measured in terms of points. A completely open, naked light shines in a full circle, or 32 points. One point is equal to 11¼ degrees. If a light is 10 points, then its arc is 10/32nds, or 5/16ths, of a circle, which is equivalent to 112 degrees. Also, there are different colored lights for each side of the boat. The red light goes on the portside, the green on the starboard side.

Under the general heading of lights, a flashlight is definitely a must.

Compass

To navigate in unfamiliar waters or in poor visibility a compass is essential. It should be purchased with a watertight cover, called a binnacle.

Spare Fuel and Tank

Unless your boat is equipped with an optional fuel gauge, a drum of spare fuel is a good idea. It must be air and watertight to prevent fumes and water, which renders the gasoline useless.

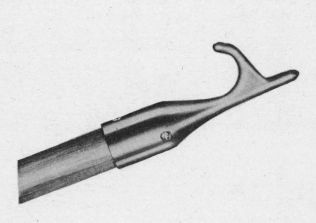

Boat Hook

Boat Hook

A boat hook is necessary for everything from fishing your hat or pet out of the water to fending off the dock. For easy stowing, a telescoping model is best. The hook part should have a cork or rubber cap when not in use to prevent accidents.

Bilge Pump

A small hand pump is good for little more than controlling a small leak and taking out rain water. Its effectiveness depends on the strength and stamina of the operator and stops him from doing anything else that may require attention. A small electric bilge pump requires no work or attention. A powerful pump can keep a boat afloat with a sizeable hole in its hull.

Radio

Beside the top 40, local stations also transmit weather reports. Part of any weather report during the boating season is the marine weather forecast, listing visibility and wind velocity. An optional attachment that can be fitted onto radios is a direction finder. The finder will point toward the source of the radio transmission. This can be an additional navigational aid.

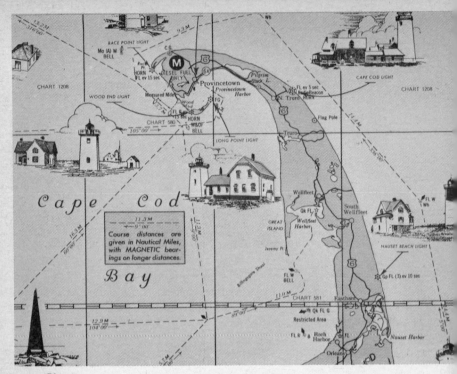

Charts

Charts are marine road maps. They are inexpensive and continually revised. Charts include information such as water depths, mileage scales, bridge clearances, buoys, lighthouses, landmarks, sunken ships, plus a great deal more. Charts are published and sold by the United States Coast and Geodetic Survey, Washington Science Center, Rockville, Maryland. A free catalog is provided just for the asking. From the catalog you can determine which charts you will need.

Bucket and Sponge

A clean boat is a tidy boat and many boat owners take pride in its appearance. A bucket, soap, sponge, and polish can be easily stored.

OPTIONAL EQUIPMENT

Optional equipment, not absolutely necessary to the boat's functioning, is for convenience. The boat may not run any better with it, but your time afloat may be more pleasurable.

Metal Reflectors

Metal reflectors are not listed among the necessary equipment because large metal craft do not need them. They are sheets of metal, sometimes collapsible, which will bounce back a radar signal. Dead in the water, a small boat may be overlooked and a wooden-hulled boat is incapable of bouncing back a signal. Metal reflectors are a good idea if your boat falls within either of these two categories.

Boarding Ladder

A boarding ladder is a convenience if the boat is used for swimming. Two-step ladders are inexpensive and hook over the transom. Three- and four-step ladders are more expensive and are used on cabin cruisers.

Windshield Wipers

Cruising in bad weather may require that an automatic electric windshield wiper be used. The cheapest electric models cost about $10.

Spotlight

Nighttime docking can be facilitated by the use of a spotlight. A good spotlight should be shock and corrosion resistant. Attach the spotlight close to the helm so that it can be operated by the pilot.

Fenders

Marine fenders are usually pieces of soft plastic threaded to a line attached to a deck cleat. They protect the hull from damage while docking. More expensive fenders are made of air-filled rubber.

Gauges

It is always useful to know at what speed you are traveling. A speedometer gives the speed in miles per hour. A tachometer is also a way of measuring speed. It records motor rpm and is an indication of how fast or how hard the motor is working. For example, to reach 35 mph quickly you may run your motor up to 3000 rpm. To maintain

Trailer

that speed once it is achieved may require only 2500 rpm. For long cruises, the motor should not be worked at a high rpm, as this makes it less efficient and wastes fuel. A middle range rpm is much more suitable. A gas gauge, indicating the amount of fuel remaining, has an obvious value.

TRAILERS

A trailer renders the boat portable. With it one can reach inland waters that are only accessible by car. Also, the boat can be transported from home to the ocean and back without the cost of a season-long dock rental.

Trailers are described in terms of their capacity. When purchasing, the weight and length of the boat should be known. Weight is the total weight of the boat, including the engine, fuel, and all the added equipment. If the total weight is within 100 pounds of the trailer capacity, then buy the next largest trailer, just to be completely safe. To figure the length, measure the centerline from bow to stern. However, a boat with a pointed bow may require a shorter trailer than one the same length with a rounder bow.

The trailer should support the hull along most of its length. Equipment stowed within the boat must be securely fastened to prevent its movement and any subsequent damage to the boat.

The best trailer hitch is mounted to the body of the car. Except for very small boats, it is not a good idea to use a fender hitch. Also, for heavy loads the trailer should have its own set of brakes. Some trailers have electrical brakes which are controlled from the inside of the car. Another type, requiring no manual labor, is the surge brake activator. As the car slows, the trailer brakes are automatically applied. This type has the advantage that in a crucial situation, the driver has just to worry about stopping his vehicle. The trailer will brake itself.

The trailer must be equipped with tail and brake lights, and turn indicators. Also, the license plate must be mounted on the back of the trailer.

Chapter 6
Insurance and Liability

It is a very good idea to insure the boat against damage and loss, and the owner against personal suit. Buying insurance is a gamble. The purchaser gambles that any loss or damage is higher than the premiums. The insurance company gambles that the total amount of money it receives from all premiums is greater than the amount of money it must pay out in claims.

There are three types of boat insurance. The least expensive is called Limited Named Perils Insurance. The policy names exactly which hazards are covered. Included are losses suffered through fire and lightning, theft of boat and motor, collision and damage to the boat if the trailer were to overturn, and windstorm on land. Only if one of these perils befalls the boat will the insurance company pay.

The second form of insurance is called Broad Named Perils Insurance. In addition to those hazards covered in the limited perils policy, it includes collision while afloat, sinking, windstorm, hurricane, and damage due to grounding.

The most expensive kind of insurance is All-Risk or Comprehensive. The policy insures the boat against just about every possible contingency. It is usually $25 to $100 deductible. Its cost is about 4 percent of the total value of the boat. The total value includes hull, motor, and all equipment.

These three types of insurance, however, do not insure the boat owner against personal suit due to loss of life or limb. Twenty-two states require some form of personal liability insurance. Usually, personal liability insurance is attached as a rider to the physical (boat)-loss policies. The extra cost frequently ranges from $10 to $40.

Coverage is usually valid only during the boating season. This extends from May 1 until November 1. For this six-month coverage, the boat owner may pay from 3 to 5 percent of his boat's total value, and he must weigh this cost against possible damage or loss. There are only two pieces of advice that can be given. First, see your insurance broker. He is probably your best source of information as to how much liability you should purchase. And second, you will not miss having insurance until you need it.

Chapter 7
Fueling

Because of the possible presence of gasoline vapors, fueling the boat must be one of the most careful, methodical tasks performed. Often it is not, and this leads to a dangerous situation, as gasoline vapors are highly flammable and, if there are enough of them, highly explosive. There can never be too much care exercised in the fueling of a boat. The following is presented as a checklist and should be religiously adhered to every time.

BEFORE FUELING

1) Check to be sure that people in the general vicinity of the fueling puts out their cigarettes, cigars, and pipes. Only after the fueling is finished, and the gasoline fumes have vanished, may smoking begin.

2) Be sure that all equipment capable of producing a spark or

Dockside Fueling

flame is off. This includes the galley. If someone is making a pot of coffee have him stop, because the fumes may find their way to the stove.

3) Close all hatches, doors, and windows. Gasoline fumes are heavier than air and can collect in the lowest parts of the boat. To prevent this from happening all entrance ways must be tightly shut.

4) Recheck the mooring lines to make positive that the boat is held fast. If they are slack, and the boat drifts, the gasoline nozzle may work its way free of the engine intake pipe and spill fuel all over the boat.

5) Have a fire extinguisher ready, just in case. The most portable types contain carbon dioxide. It will snuff out the fire, leaving behind no residue. Also, check the fire extinguisher to be sure it has the correct pressure.

WHILE FUELING

1) Place the fuel nozzle in contact with the engine intake pipe. The motor is grounded, and by placing the fuel nozzle against the fill pipe, it too will be grounded. This will help prevent the formation of a static spark, which could ignite the fuel.

2) Avoid spilling any fuel. This usually occurs when the tank is full and the excess spills onto the deck. The best advice is to be aware just how much fuel is needed and then pump in a little less because gasoline expands.

AFTER FUELING

1) If any fuel has been spilled, wipe up or hose down the deck.

2) Open all hatches, doors, and windows. If fumes are lingering, the resultant breeze will help to dispel them. Allow at least five minutes for the boat to air.

3) Check for fumes. There is no better fume-detecting device than the nose. Sniff around the outside of the boat, as well as around the motor and fuel lines. If the boat is inboard powered, turn on the blowers.

4) Start the engine only after feeling assured that no gasoline fumes are present.

5) Maintain the fuel system according to the manufacturer's recommendations and inspect it periodically. It is amazing what a well-trained eye can tell at a glance. For example, if the fuel line fittings feel damp, it means that gasoline is escaping and evaporating.

BUYING GASOLINE

There is little difference between marine and automobile gasoline. Marine gasoline costs a few cents a gallon more. This is in no small way due to the fact that it is a seasonable business and the trucker may find it a little more difficult to approach the fueling station storage tanks on the water's edge. If you want to save a few cents, buy some good sturdy metal carrying cans and fill them up when you do your car. However, remember that gasoline weighs about six pounds a gallon.

Chapter 8
Boat Handling

Unlike an automobile, a boat turns from the stern. If the boat is steered to the right, the bow will move slightly to the right but the stern will kick much further to the left. In just about every maneuver, it is the stern that must be watched out for.

Most inboards have right-handed propellers, which rotate clockwise when viewed from astern. Because of this the stern has a natural tendency to swing momentarily to the left. It is a good idea, whenever possible, to circle to the right, as the natural inclination of the stern makes for an easier right turn.

Learning to handle a boat takes skill and practice, but it is a task easily mastered.

LEAVING THE DOCK

Depending on whether the dock is crowded or not, there are two methods of launching the boat.

Launching from an Open Dock

1) Cast-off all lines. Check to be sure there are no mooring lines to hold the boat.

2) Turn the wheel or outboard very slightly away from the dock. Turning hard in the direction of the open water will swing the stern into the dock. The direction taken should almost be straight ahead.

3) Turn toward the open water only after the boat is one or two hull lengths from the dock. This will allow the stern enough room to swing freely about.

Launching from a Crowded Dock

1) Leave the bow line securely tied. Cast-off all other lines. This method will pivot the boat around the bow.

2) Turn the wheel or outboard in the direction of the open water.

3) Go forward slowly. The stern will turn away from the dock and face toward the open water.

4) Cast-off the bow line.

5) Center the wheel or outboard and put the motor in reverse, enabling the boat to back out into open water.

ANCHORS AND ANCHORING

Of the several different types of anchors, three are best suited to the needs of powerboats. The yachtsman's anchor is large and heavy, and because of this is appropriate mainly for big craft. It performs best in sheltered and slow waters. The mushroom anchor is used as a temporary hold for small fishing boats. Also, it is effective as a permanent anchor for docking over soft, mudlike bottoms. The most popular anchors currently in use are the patent models. Both of these, the Danforth and Northill anchors, are light and collapsible for easy storage. Once dug in, both have good holding power.

The actual anchor line is called a rode. The length of line is a scope. The larger the scope, the more effectively the anchor will hold to the bottom. A judgment must be made of the current and wind strength before deciding on the best scope. Under good conditions, a scope three times longer than the bottom depth is sufficient. In an extreme wind or current, a scope ten times the bottom depth is recommended.

The process of dropping and setting the anchor is easily mastered. First, head directly into the wind or current with the motor in neutral. As the boat stops, carefully let out the rode until it goes slack. This means that the anchor has touched bottom and, if the rode is marked, make a mental notation of water depth. Never toss the anchor from the boat. This may foul the line. To set the anchor, reverse the boat gently until it is felt that the flukes (the part of the anchor that imbeds itself) are dug in and holding.

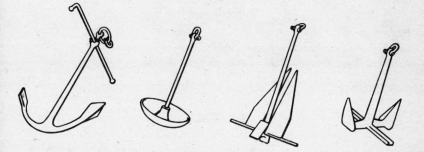

Anchors: Yachtsman's, Mushroom, Danforth, Northill

BEACHING

Because the motor can be raised out of harm's way, an outboard can be brought directly into the shore for camping or picnicking. Never even consider beaching an inboard.

Choose a spot which appears to have a soft, rock-free bottom. Raise the outboard until the propeller is just barely beneath the waterline and send the bow onto the beach. If necessary raise the outboard completely out of the water just before contact. To beach the craft securely, jump out and physically haul the bow onto the beach.

It is a good idea to attach the bow line to a nearby tree to prevent the bow from slipping. If in a tidal situation, toss the anchor well off the stern. This way if the tide goes out, leaving the boat high and dry, the hull can be hauled into the water by kedging, or pulling the boat toward the anchor.

Beached Boat

TOWING

The length of the tow line is the most important factor in successful towing. Of course, the tow line should be strong enough to take the stress.

One end of the line should be tied to a stern cleat on the towing vessel and the other end should fasten low onto the bow of the boat being towed. Let the line out until the desired traveling speed is reached. Small light boats are efficiently towed if they ride just backward of the second wake. Heavy boats are suitably towed if they ride just forward of the top of either the first or second wake.

Towing

DOCKING

Docking a boat takes practice and, the first few times it is attempted, do not be discouraged if it is done sloppily. When approaching the dock, move slowly, just fast enough to maintain control of the boat. It is probably best to stop the boat a few lengths from the dock and then proceed by alternately putting the motor in

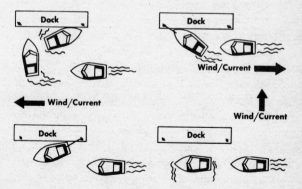

Diagram of Docking Approaches

forward and neutral.

Depending on the current or wind direction, there are several ways of approaching the mooring. Never head into the current or wind as they will either push the boat past the dock or directly into it. Be sure the fenders are attached.

If wind and current are not a factor, the usual method is to approach the dock at about a 30 degree angle. Turn the wheel slowly until the boat is parallel to the mooring, reverse gears to stop the boat, and secure the lines.

If the wind and current are from the leeward (wind off the dock), then approach at a sharp angle until the bow makes contact, and secure the bow line. Next turn the wheel away from the dock, put the motor in forward, and the stern will swing into the dock.

When approaching the mooring from the weather side (wind toward the dock), halt the boat a few feet aft and parallel to the berth, and the boat will drift into the dock.

DECK LINES

A small boat needs only three different types of deck lines for mooring. They are the bow line, the stern line, and a set of spring lines.

The bow and stern lines are used for securing the fore and aft to the dock. In most docking situations in which the boat is tied up for short periods or where there is quiet water, only the bow and stern lines are necessary. Just in case, however, the bow and stern lines should be fastened to the dock using a bowline knot.

The spring lines prevent fore and aft movement of the boat when tied to the dock. They fit over the bow or stern cleat and, respectively, run aft or forward to the dock cleat. They should be quite long. A spring line about as long as the boat is ample enough for any situation. The most secure manner of tying a boat is to use both port and starboard spring lines, as well as the bow and stern lines. If the docking area is subject to tides, the spring lines should be slack to allow for the rise and fall of the boat.

KNOTS

To securely fasten the boat to the dock or to the anchor, a knowledge of knots is necessary. Five basic types are sufficient for just about every tying need.

Bowline

The bowline knot is used for making a permanent loop which can be slipped over a pier piling. The knot is made by making a loop (bite), then bringing the free end back through the loop, around the line, and back through the loop again.

Half Hitch

One of the easiest knots to make for securing a line to a piling is the half hitch. Drape the line around the piling. Bring the free end over and under the long end and then over and under itself and through the loop.

Clove Hitch

The clove hitch is a quickly made knot used to attach a line temporarily to a dock piling. A second loop is made with the free end and also placed over the piling. When a clove hitch is strained it tends to tighten, making it hard to free.

Square

A square knot is used for tying together two ends. Loop one line and then bring the second up through and under.

Fisherman's Bend

The fisherman's bend is an excellent knot for attaching a line to a buoy or anchor. Loop the line twice around the eyelet. Bring the free end across the line, through the loop, and then again around the line.

Chapter 9
Boating Laws and Rules of The Road

REGISTERING AND NUMBERING THE BOAT

A boat owner does not need an operator's license to be able to pilot his craft. However, he must register his boat with the appropriate authorities. Failure to register can result in a $50 fine.

Most states handle the registration and assign the boat a number. It is a good idea to become familiar with the registration procedure before purchasing a first boat. Usually there is a fee and the registration must be renewed every three years. In Alaska, New Hampshire, and Washington, the boat owner registers with the Coast Guard, which then assigns the boat a number.

It is the owner's responsibility to affix the boat's number to both sides of the bow. The number must be at least three inches high and be in a legible color. Upon sale of the boat, the registration-issuing agency must be notified.

The boat buyer does not have to demonstrate skill or competence in boat handling to get his boat registered. A simple application form and the fee is all that is necessary. However, it is advisable that the beginning skipper apply for boating instruction to the U.S. Coast Guard Auxiliary or the United States Power Squadrons.

U.S. COAST GUARD AUXILIARY

The U.S. Coast Guard Auxiliary offers three basic courses on handling and seamanship. All are given free to the public and are designed specifically for the beginner.

The course in outboard handling consists of one lesson on the fundamental rules of boat handling, equipment requirements, and courtesy afloat.

A slightly more extensive course, covering three lessons, is given on safe boating. It includes aids to navigation and safety rules for both inboard and outboard operators.

The eight-lesson course on basic seamanship is the most complete given by the Auxiliary. It covers marlinspike seamanship, safety, and navigation. Upon successful completion, the U.S. Coast Guard Auxiliary Basic Seamanship Certificate is awarded.

UNITED STATES POWER SQUADRONS

The United States Power Squadrons are an organization composed of boatmen. They offer an extensive course of twelve lectures covering all phases of boat operation. For information about local classes contact USPS Headquarters, P.O. Box 510, Englewood, New Jersey 07631.

Overloaded Boat

LOADING THE BOAT

It is highly dangerous to overload a boat with passengers or gear. Many boat manufacturers now install a capacity plate showing the recommended weight capacity both in terms of number of people and total weight, including passengers, motor, fuel, and gear. These values are recommended for fair weather. It is not a smart idea to ignore the manufacturer's recommendations. They have tested their boat and know better than you its limitations.

If the boat is not equipped with a capacity plate, the total weight it can carry can be roughly calculated using a simple formula. Multiply the overall length of the boat, its maximum width, and its minimum effective depth by 7.5. The answer will give some idea of the total carrying capacity in pounds of the boat.

Weather and water conditions must be taken into account. If the water is rough, the number of recommended passengers and the total weight must be reduced.

ACCIDENTS

Boat accidents include personal and property damage due to collision, flood, fire, explosion, and capsizing. Under law, the boat owner involved in an accident must stop and render assistance. He must also identify himself and his boat to the other party. However, his assistance is limited by the fact that he should not endanger himself or his craft. Boats in the vicinity of an accident are not to leave the scene and should render assistance if possible.

The boat operator must submit a written report within a specified period of time to the Coast Guard or to the state with which his boat is registered. In case of loss of life, the report must be filed within 48 hours after the accident. If there is property damage totaling more than $100 or serious injury, the report must be submitted within five days. It is always safer to report an accident if there is a question as to whether the damages might be in excess of $100. Failure to report can result in stiff penalties.

RIGHT-OF-WAY

There are no traffic lights or stop signals on the watery road. It is therefore imperative that one learn and use the common rules of the road. If unsure of the particular situation, remember that safety and courtesy come first. The most that could be lost is a few minutes and, in pleasurable boating, time should not be all that important.

The first rule is that boats without motors, sail and oar boats, always have the right-of-way with respect to powerboats, they are not as easily maneuverable as motorboats and can be severely hampered by a wake.

A boat having the right-of-way is termed the privileged vessel and it maintains its course. The craft that must veer off or slow down is known as the burdened vessel. Certain horn and whistle signals are used to signal intention. The other craft will respond with the same signal, indicating that the maneuver is understood.

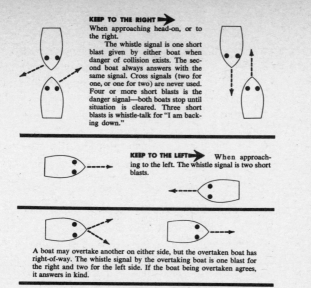

KEEP TO THE RIGHT When approaching head-on, or to the right.

The whistle signal is one short blast given by either boat when danger of collision exists. The second boat always answers with the same signal. Cross signals (two for one, or one for two) are never used. Four or more short blasts is the danger signal—both boats stop until situation is cleared. Three short blasts is whistle-talk for "I am backing down."

KEEP TO THE LEFT When approaching to the left. The whistle signal is two short blasts.

A boat may overtake another on either side, but the overtaken boat has right-of-way. The whistle signal by the overtaking boat is one blast for the right and two for the left side. If the boat being overtaken agrees, it answers in kind.

When crossing, the boat to the right of the other (privileged) has right-of-way. Boats with right-of-way should hold their course and speed. The "burdened" boat should slow down, stop, or turn to pass to the rear of the boat on the right. The whistle signal (first given by the "privileged" boat) is one blast.

Diagram of Rules of the Road

Possibly the most dangerous situation exists when two boats approach each other head on. Both boats should immediately steer to starboard (right) and pass each other portside to portside (on the left). One short blast of the horn or whistle is customary. In addition, out of courtesy both boats should slow to prevent their wakes from interfering with one another. In very open water, where the approaching boats are separated by several lengths, the signals are unnecessary.

When two boats approach each other at right angles, on a collision course, the boat on the right is the privileged vessel and has the right-of-way. The burdened vessel should either slow or swing aft of the other boat. One blast of the horn or whistle and its reply signals that both boats understand the situation.

In a passing situation, the boat to be overtaken always has the right-of-way. The faster boat signals his intentions by either one blast of the horn or whistle if he is going to pass on the starboard side, or two blasts if on the port. In this case, it is very important that the passing boat wait for a reply from the slower boat, which will then slide to the other side giving the other more room to pass. Also the reply means that the slower boat will not suddenly turn into the faster boat's path.

A boat leaving port has no rights whatsoever until it reaches open water. It should proceed slowly and be prepared to wait its turn. One long blast is sounded.

A dangerous situation exists if the other boat does not reply to the horn or whistle signal. Without a reply, it should not be assumed that its operator understands or is even aware of your intention. Always put safety first. If need be, concede the right-of-way. Four blasts of the horn or whistle indicates that there is possible danger. Both boats should slow or stop and iron out the difficulty. Never assume that a signal is understood until a reply is given.

NIGHT LIGHTS

Night or running lights are required equipment on boats underway from sunset to sunrise. They indicate the approximate bearing of another vessel in relation to your own.

A red light is placed on the portside of the bow, a green on the starboard. If, when traveling at night, a red light is visible, it indicates that the two boats are approaching each other at approximate right angles, and that the other is the privileged vessel, having the right-of-way. The burdened craft would show its green light to the other.

For night running become familiar with the Coast Guard regulations concerning proper lighting. Given two knowledgeable skippers there is no reason why after dark cruising should be any different than in daylight. Remember: The rules of the road always apply.

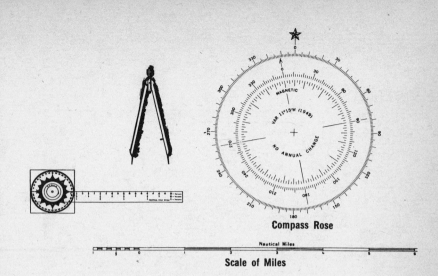

Compass Rose

Nautical Miles

Scale of Miles

Chapter 10
Piloting and Navigating

Chart, compass, and parallel rule are the only equipment necessary for simple navigation. Exact charts of U.S. coastal and inland waters are prepared by and available from either the Corps of Engineers or the Coast and Geodetic Survey Office. The charts contain all the information needed to successfully navigate in U.S. waters. Figures indicating the average low water measurement for the area are listed. Other details include the locations and types of buoys, danger areas which may contain shoals or rocks, and prominent landmarks, such as church steeples and factory smokestacks. Vertical lines show longitude (true north—south) and horizontal lines latitude (true east—west).

Because of all the information they contain, abbreviations and symbols are necessary on charts. For example, a diamond-shaped symbol indicates a buoy. A black diamond shows the location of a black buoy, a magenta diamond, a red buoy. A triangle indicates a day beacon and the abbreviation "Bn" appears nearby.

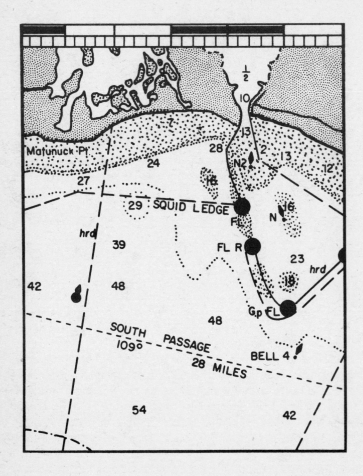

Chart

Compass

An adequate navigating compass is graduated in units of 5 to 10 degrees. Compasses point toward the magnetic north pole, not to the geographical north pole. The magnetic north pole is not in the same place as the geographic north pole. In addition, depending on the location of the compass, the degree difference between the magnetic and geographic north poles varies. This occurs because the earth is a sphere. If the earth were flat, then the angle between the two would never change. The location of the geographic north pole is a constant. The location of the magnetic north pole is also constant, but the relation of an observer on a spherical surface to it varies. The difference in degrees between the direction in which the compass points and the geographic north pole is called compass variation.

PLOTTING COURSES

Charts are laid out on the basis of the geographic north pole. Knowing the amount of variation at a particular location between the magnetic pole-seeking compass and the geographic north pole, it is possible to plot a course. The compass rose on a chart indicates the variation. The outer circle points in the direction of true north (the geographic north pole). The inner circle indicates the direction of the magnetic north pole. Assume a course of due east is desired. Geographically, the direction is 90 degrees. However if the variation is 10 degrees, then in order to head due east a compass heading of 100 degrees must be followed.

A slightly more complicated case occurs if the plotting is done between two points and then the direction determined. Using a parallel rule, draw a line between the two points. Extend the rule until it passes through the center of the nearest compass rose. The place at which it bisects the inner circle is the compass heading needed to pilot between the two points.

Frequently, it is not possible because of obstacles to travel in a straight line, and several compass headings are needed. The method used is hopping from buoy to buoy. When the first buoy is reached, the direction is altered until the next is sighted, and so on. If there are not enough buoy markers along the desired route, or if their location leads to a roundabout course, then knowing the speed of the boat is important. For example, suppose the first leg of the journey is to be taken at a compass heading of 87 degrees for 3 miles, and the next section at a heading of 115 degrees for 6 miles. A boat traveling at 30 MPH will do the 3-mile leg in 6 minutes and then, turning to a heading of 115 degrees, proceed for 12 minutes to arrive at its destination.

Coastal navigation is accomplished by sightings taken from land objects. Assume there is a visible church spire and a factory storage tank along the coast. Using your eye, quickly sight up through the compass their direction. Allowing for variance, draw a line on the chart through the landmarks at the angle indicated by the compass. The point at which these lines intersect is the approximate position of the boat.

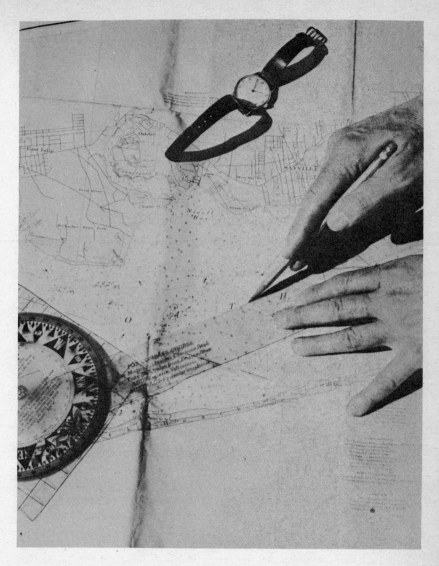

Someone in the Process of Charting

Compasses are influenced by the proximity of steel and iron. The error caused by their presence is called deviation. Most compasses are adjustable to remove the deviation.

MEASURING TIME, SPEED AND DISTANCE

Chart distances are measured in nautical miles. A nautical mile is 1.15 larger than a statute mile. If the speedometer on the boat is in statute miles-per-hour, it is a good idea to make a conversion table showing statute miles-per-hour and their equivalent in nautical miles-per-hour.

To measure the expected time of a trip, add the distances plotted on the chart. Every chart contains a key showing the relationship between inches and miles. Divide the distance by the expected average speed of the boat. For example, a 30-mile trip at an average speed of 20 MPH will take 1½ hours. (Speed multiplied by time equals distance.)

Speedometer error can be measured by running the boat over a course the length of which is known. Many shorelines have stakes indicating a measured mile. Run the boat up to its usual cruising speed and, using a stopwatch, record the time elapsed from marker to marker. Because performance can be affected by current and wind, it is a good idea to run the course at least three times. Average the time in seconds and divide the result into 3,600 (the number of seconds in one hour). The answer is the actual speed of the boat over the measured mile. The difference between the speedometer reading and the actual speed, if any, is the amount of speedometer error that can be expected at cruising speed.

TIDES AND CURRENTS

Tides are caused by the gravitational pull of the moon and, to a lesser extent, the sun. During each 24 hours there are two flood and two ebb tides. The moon rises 50 minutes later every day, and because

Low tide.

High tide.

Effect of Tides

of this tides occur 50 minutes later each day.

The relative position of the sun and moon also influences tides. Spring tides occur when the moon and sun are in a direct line (at new and full moon) and result in very high tides bordering on flooding. The opposite effect occurs when the moon and sun are at right angles to the earth (first and last quarters of the moon), producing exceptionally low tides, called neap tides.

Tidal flow results in currents. Tides are the up and down motion of the water; currents are horizontal water movement. When leaving a dock during a 2 MPH current caused by an ebb tide, the boat will travel 2 MPH faster in relation to the bottom. The reverse is also true. A boat heading into a 2 MPH current will move that much slower. Currents are more difficult than tides to measure, as they can be influenced by wind and flooding. Tables which list currents for a particular area should not be assumed to be completely accurate.

In piloting a boat, the effect of current should be taken into account. For example, a 2-hour north—south journey in a 2 MPH east—west current will result in a landing 4 miles west of the expected destination. In such a situation, the boat must be steered in an easterly arc, eliminating the effect of the current pushing the boat toward the west.

AIDS TO NAVIGATION

Buoyage of the United States

Buoys are marine signposts. Depending on their color, number, shape, and characteristics, they indicate the presence of danger zones or merely show the best course to steer.

Used as navigational aids, buoys show the proper way of entering and leaving a harbor. Red buoys are always even-numbered and have conical shapes. They are called "nun" buoys. Nun buoys should always be kept to the starboard when entering a harbor. The nautical expression "red right returning" is used to remind the pilot that red buoys are passed on your right. Black buoys are odd-numbered, and called "cans" because of their shape. Black buoys should be off the port when proceeding into a harbor. The combination of red buoys to the starboard and black buoys off the port clearly define a marine roadway. When leaving the docking area toward the open sea the positions are reversed. Red buoys should be off the port, and black buoys off the starboard. The same lane can be used for both incoming and outgoing boats. It is a good idea when coming into the docking area to keep to the right, near the red buoys.

There are other types of buoys. A buoy with red and black horizontal stripes indicates an obstruction or a junction. It can be passed on either side if used to show a danger zone. An obstruction buoy used as a junction marker has a red or black top band symbolizing the direction of the best channel. From seaward, the red top acts as a regular red buoy and should be kept to the starboard. By doing this, a channel on the buoy's left is indicated. The opposite is true if the buoy has a black top stripe. Channel buoys are black-and-white vertically striped buoys and may appear in any shape. They inform the pilot that he is steering too far toward the center of the channel. Range lights are generally visible from one direction and, when aligned, they indicate a safe course. They may be fixed or flashing white, red, or green lights.

Lighthouses and Lightships

Lighthouses serve to warn the pilot of danger spots or guide him into harbor entrances. Each lighthouse is painted differently and has its own characteristic color of light or frequency of flash. Marine charts describe each lighthouse so that one may not be mistaken for another. They are usually installed with fog and radio-beacon signals.

Lightships are moveable lighthouses marking harbor entrances or shoals. Also, like lighthouses, they have their own distinct characteristics. The hull is painted red with the station name in white on both sides.

FLAGS AND THEIR MEANING

A set of International Code signal flags contains 40 flags: 26 letters, ten numbers, three repeaters, and a code and answering flag. Most pleasure boaters do not carry a set of flags, and it probably is not necessary to have them. Flags are an international language, and they may be needed to converse with a foreign vessel. All danger signals consist of two flags, the uppermost being the first letter. The following are some of the most important signals:

AE: I must abandon my vessel.
AM: There has been an accident. I need a doctor.
AP: I am aground.
AT: I am aground and require immediate assistance.
DQ: I am on fire and require immediate assistance.
DV: I have sprung a leak.
FR: I require a boat. Man overboard.
HP: Submarines are exercising. Navigate with caution.
JD: You are standing into danger.
JZ: I have a damaged rudder and cannot steer.
LI: I am disabled.
LO: My engines are disabled.
LP: My steering gear is disabled.
LV: I am in distress for want of fuel.
MJ: Have you a doctor?
PQ: I have sprung a leak and require immediate assistance.
PT: I require a pilot.
RH: Message has been received.
ST: I require a police boat.
TH: I have lost my propeller.
TK: I require provisions urgently.
TZ: My radio is not working.
WU: What course should I steer to make nearest land?
YJ: I require water immediately.

THE PHONETIC ALPHABET AND MORSE CODE

Because of an accent or an emergency stress situation, it may not be possible to distinctly communicate valuable life-saving information. A phonetic code can be used in these circumstances to spell out the message. Morse code is also used to communicate a distress signal. The alphabet equivalent in phonetic language and Morse code is

A Alpha . _
B Bravo _ . . .
C Charlie _ . _ .
D Delta _ . .
E Echo .
F Foxtrot . . _ .
G Golf _ _ .
H Hotel . . . .
I India . .
J Juliet . _ _ _
K Kilo _ . _
L Lima . _ . .
M Mike _ _

N November _ .
O Oscar _ _ _
P Papa . _ _ .
Q Quebec _ _ . _
R Romeo . _ .
S Sierra . . .
T Tango _
U Uniform . . _
V Victor . . . _
W Whisky . _ _
X X ray _ . . _
Y Yankee _ . _ _
Z Zulu _ _ . .

Chapter 11
Weather

A radio on a boat means access to the latest marine forecast. But if the batteries run down or the radio is damaged, future changes in the weather can still be determined. Nature supplies indications of continued fair weather or brewing storms. The sky, sun, moon, and clouds are all signals of what is to come.

FORECASTING FROM NATURE

Weather in the United States generally moves from west to east. The sun rises in the east and sets in the west. By noting the sky at sunset it is possible to get a preview of the next day's weather. For example, a red sky at sunset presages a fair tomorrow. Approaching clouds interfering with the setting sun may result in a bright yellow sunset, indicating that the next day is going to be windy. A pale yellow sunset may mean rain. A sunset hidden by white clouds indicates that a storm is brewing.

The color of the sunrise is also an important sign. A red sky at sunrise presages bad weather, and if the sun rises out of a gray horizon, fair weather is probably in the offing.

When the moon has a halo, its light is diffusing through a cloud cover. Rain or wind should be expected.

There is no need to learn the different names of clouds, because each name stands for a certain type or description. Delicate fluffy clouds hold little water and indicate fair weather and moderate breezes. The darker the clouds, the greater the coming wind. Small black clouds omen rain. Light clouds moving fast under darker heavier clouds foretell of wind and rain. Thunderstorms usually arrive as gray clouds with bulbous tops. The rapid formation of dense vertical clouds can also indicate a thunderstorm.

STORM SIGNALS

Storm signals are flown at the Coast Guard installations as well as at other locations. It is a very good idea to become familiar with their placement and their meaning.

A single red pennant by day and a red light over a white light at night are small craft warnings. They are shown when winds over 38 MPH are forecast. Winds this strong make small craft operations dangerous.

Gale warnings consist of two red pennants or a white light over a red light and indicate winds from 38 to 54 MPH.

A whole gale warning is transmitted by a single square red flag with a black center by day, and two red lights at night. Whole gale winds range from 55 to 73 MPH.

The most feared pennant is the hurricane warning. It consists of two red flags with black centers in daylight, and a white light sandwiched between two red at night. Winds in excess of 74 MPH are expected.

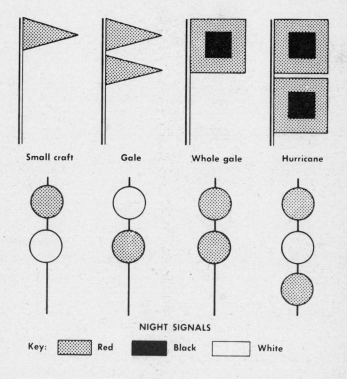

Small craft   Gale   Whole gale   Hurricane

NIGHT SIGNALS

Key: Red   Black   White

Storm Signals

Fog bells are required on certain boats so that they can sound the proper signal when under way in fog. There are automatic fog signal devices available, the cost of which, of course, is appreciably higher.

FOG

Because it limits visibility, fog is one of the main enemies of the boater. Fog is usually the result of a hot humid air mass being cooled as it passes over land or water. In daylight, frequently the fog is burned away as the sun warms the water and land. By steering into warmer water, it is possible to avoid fog.

However, it is not easy to find warmer water, and the usual situation is to travel in the fog. In fog, exercise the utmost caution. The appearance of another boat or obstruction can be quite sudden. It is important to travel at a safe speed which will permit stopping in about half the distance of visibility. If you have a fog bell, use it. Upon hearing another vessel's bell immediately stop until it is possible to discern its direction and distance. Since you cannot see everywhere at once, ask all passengers to act as lookouts. Another good idea is to constantly keep track of the boat's position on the chart. If you find yourself lost, anchor the boat and wait for the fog to lift. Even when anchored, continually sound the fog bell.

READING THE WATER

Accurate water reading is gained through experience. On the open sea, the water responds to the push of the wind. For example, a light breeze of 4 to 7 MPH results in about 6-inch wavelets with unbroken crests. A strong breeze of 25 to 31 MPH causes the formation of large 13-foot waves with white foam crests.

In rough weather, as the boat approaches the shore, the waves will begin to swell and break. Coming toward the docking area from the leeward side is considerably easier and safer, as the land, to some extent, shelters the water from the full effect of the wind. It can be a frightening experience to approach the shore with the wind at your back. When in high waves, do not attempt to outrace them to the shore. The boat will go up the wave, down over the crest, and the bow will plunge straight under the water. Try to have the boat's speed about the same as the wave velocity. This way it is possible to ride the same wave position all the way to shore.

River reading is different from ocean reading. There are many more indicators of the water's flow in a river. Current direction can be seen by the movement of floating debris and in the darker color of fast flowing deep water. Underwater obstacles can be spotted as the water ripples around them. Swift downstream flowing water narrowing over a rock bottom forms a V-shaped channel. Always steer in the center of the channel; it contains the deeper water. An upstream V-shaped channel should be avoided entirely. It indicates a large obstacle that is close to the surface.

When passing by a tributary, attempt to keep heading with the main stream. Frequently, a tributary carries mud and deposits the sediment when it comes in contact with a larger body of water. The quieter water off to the sides is shallower due to the deposits.

The best way to run a river is to always steer with the darker deep water. If the river bends, the deepest water will be at the outer edge of the curve.

After a storm always be on the lookout for debris that may have been washed into the river. Proceed at slow speed so that if an object is struck, it will merely glance off the hull.

Chapter 12
In Case of Emergency

Boating ranks as one of the safest of all the outdoor sports. But accidents do happen. When they do, the captain should have already rehearsed his actions in his mind. Boating accidents include fire, explosion, sinking, capsizing, collision, drowning, and running aground. When they occur, they can be serious. Inadequately manufactured boats and motors are certainly a cause of accidents, but the main culprit is irresponsible operation. Not bothering to learn the rules of the road and the significance of buoy markers, overloading, operating the boat while drunk, and not carrying sufficient safety equipment are irresponsible acts that can result in injury.

When an accident occurs, the first thing to remember is not to panic. Usually, injury and property damage can be kept to a minimum if the right action is immediately taken.

DISTRESS SIGNALS

There are many ways of communicating distress to another boat or to the Coast Guard. An upside down flag or ensign, a white cloth flying from the highest point on the boat, the rapid sounding of a horn, bell or whistle are common signals that can be easily noticed by another boat. Recently, the Coast Guard has inaugurated a new distress signal for small boats. Slowly, outstretched arms are raised and lowered to the side. A nighttime distress signal can be sent by signaling SOS (3 dots, 3 dashes, 3 dots) with the boat's spotlight. Also, flares can be used. If a boat is seen using any of these signals, come to its assistance immediately.

Radiotelephone

The Coast Guard can be contacted by radiotelephone at 2182 kc. All Coast Guard rescue stations, marine operators, and many boat operators maintain a constant vigilance on this frequency. If in grave or immediate danger, the call should be preceded by the word "MAYDAY" spoken three times. The caller should be ready to supply the following information:

1) Boat's name and radio call letters

2) The vessel's position in latitude and longitude or true bearing and distance in nautical miles from a widely known geographical point.

3) Nature of the distress or difficulty

4) Kind of assistance desired

5) Number of persons aboard and the condition of any injured

6) Whether the vessel is in immediate danger

7) Description of the boat, including length and type, color of hull and superstructure

8) Listening frequency.

Boat on Fire

FIRE

Fire is the greatest single danger facing the boat owner. In Chapter 7, we discussed the fire prevention steps to be taken while fueling. Every boat should be equipped with a fire extinguisher and a pail or bucket. Periodically, check the fire extinguisher to see whether it is up to pressure or weight, and replace any cracked or broken hoses. The fire extinguisher and bucket should be easily accessible, and all adults should know where they are stored.

An above decks fire should be approached from upwind, allowing the breeze to carry the extinguishing substance into the flame. Also, it is a good idea to stop the boat to prevent the fire from being fanned by the wind. Try to keep the fire downwind from the rest of the boat to stop it from spreading. If the fire is toward the stern, turn the bow into the wind. If forward, turn the stern to the wind. A fire can be smothered by wetting a blanket or other large piece of cloth and tossing it on top of the flame. If the burning object is moveable, throw it over the side.

A fire below decks or in the engine compartment is a much more serious matter. Close all doors, windows, and hatches in an attempt to rob the fire of oxygen. Gasoline is highly flammable and explosive. In case of an engine fire immediately turn off the fuel supply. To prevent the fuel tanks from getting hot and vaporizing the gasoline into explosive fumes, continually wet the tanks until they are about the same temperature as the outside air.

LEAKING HULL

A leaking hull can be the direct effect of a collision with submerged or floating objects, or another boat. Minor leaks are usually due to the opening of a hull seam or the failure of a fitting or hose. Unless there is a major hole in the hull, the craft can be saved and kept afloat by quick action.

Standard equipment should include a small electric pump or a hand pump. However, it is a good idea to have a hand pump in addition to the electric pump, since the power might fail. At the first sign of a leak start the pump and head immediately toward land. Have all passengers don their life jackets.

Frequently the leak can be easily located, but do not hesitate to rip up the floorboards to find the hole. When the leak is found stuff anything available into the hole to stem the flow. A piece of plywood, tin, or canvas should be nailed over the plug. It will not be watertight, but it will help gain more time.

If the boat is rammed, stop immediately. It may be necessary to travel in reverse if the bow is damaged. This will help reduce the flow, making repairs easier.

A damaged fitting or hose is also a cause of leaks. Since the hole is usually circular, a wooden plug can be used. Frequently, the water intake hose for the engine is damaged or split. A spare hose can be attached to the engine and run back through the original hole.

Man Overboard

MAN OVERBOARD

Even if the person is a good swimmer, speed is important in rescuing someone who has fallen overboard. Immediately turn the stern of the boat away from the man so he cannot become caught in the propeller. Next throw him a life preserver. While keeping the man in sight, maneuver the boat so as to approach him from downwind. If there are high waves an upwind approach may cause you to lose sight of the man. With the motor off, help the man into the boat. The most stable place to board a small boat is over the stern or bow. Boarding from the sides may tip or capsize the boat.

In the above description it is a man that falls overboard. But more often than not, it is a child. It is a very good idea to have all children wear life jackets. This will help them stay afloat while the boat is manuevered for the rescue.

ABANDONING SHIP

Most boats, even if gutted by a fire, will stay afloat. Always stay in the vicinity of the ship. It is far easier for help to spot a boat floundering than locate a person swimming. Also, remember that visibility over water is usually quite good and the land that appears close may be beyond your swimming ability to reach it. Before abandoning ship, send out whatever distress signals you can. However, when it is time to jump, jump.

EMERGENCY FIRST AID

Every boat should have an easily accessible first-aid kit adequate enough to treat all the passengers that may be aboard. Manufactured kits should be supplemented by items advised by the family doctor. In addition, a manual, such as *First-Aid Textbook* by the American Red Cross, should be part of the equipment. Standard drugs, like aspirin, antiseptic, rubbing alcohol, and smelling salts must also be carried. Depending on the particular area you cruise, certain other drugs might be needed. For example, if swimming in an area which has poisonous water snakes, a snakebite kit is necessary.

Artificial Respiration

If caught in time, it is possible to revive someone who has stopped breathing. Mouth-to-mouth respiration is probably the best way to effect a revival. A plastic resuscitator tube can be used instead of direct contact. Artificial respiration should be given for at least four hours. Frequently, the recovery is only temporary and the patient should be watched for a relapse. The following steps are for mouth-to-mouth respiration:

Artificial Respiration

1) Loosen the clothing and put a blanket over the victim.

2) Check to see if the mouth is blocked. Remove anything, such as chewing gum or mucus.

3) Tilt the head back until the chin points upward.

4) Push the jaw open until it is jutting out.

5) Put the resuscitator tube into the victim's mouth and pinch the nose shut. If using direct mouth-to-mouth contact, pinch the nostrils shut.

6) Blow into the victim's mouth. Remove your mouth, wait for the victim to return the air, and then repeat.

Adults should receive 12 breaths per minute; children 20 shallow breaths per minute.

Shock

A victim of any type of accident can instantly go into shock, and sometimes shock can result in death. Symptoms of shock include gray face, pale lips, blue nails, a fast but weak pulse, a cold sweat, shaking and chills, extreme tiredness, and nausea or vomiting. All of these symptoms may or may not be present in any one individual. It is enough that some exist to assume shock.

Treat shock by keeping the victim warm. Lay him down so that his head is lower than his legs. If you can get the victim to drink, administer hot tea or coffee. Do not force him to drink if he is unconscious. To revive the victim, use smelling salts. In case of a head injury or excessive bleeding, do not give a stimulant.

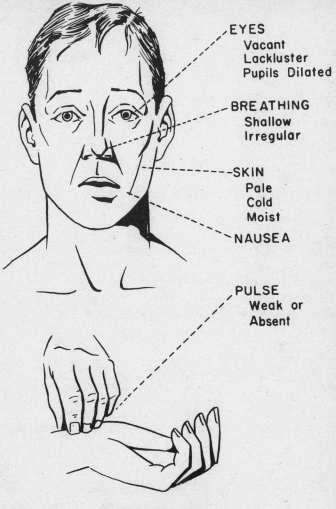

EYES
Vacant
Lackluster
Pupils Dilated

BREATHING
Shallow
Irregular

SKIN
Pale
Cold
Moist

NAUSEA

PULSE
Weak or
Absent

SYMPTOMS OF SHOCK

Chapter 13
Maintenance and Upkeep

A boat can provide years of enjoyment if properly maintained. It is valueless to have a boat that is spotless and ignore the basic upkeep routine for motor and hull. Readying the boat for carefree cruising can be time-consuming, but a lot more time can be spent lying dead in the water awaiting help.

BEFORE LAUNCHING

Even if the boat is brand new, there are a few procedures that should be accomplished before launching. A boat stored over the winter is likely to need most or all of the maintenance described next.

Hull Maintenance

The exterior of the hull should be scrubbed with mild detergent and fresh water. Any barnacles still remaining should be scraped off. Make sure that all hull fastenings, such as cleats, are tight. Replace any that appear bent or corroded. The sacrificial zinc anodes, which help to prevent a metal hull from corroding in salt water, should also be replaced. All parts of the steering mechanism must be examined, and adjusted if necessary. File down any propeller nicks. Before launching be sure that all bilge openings are shut.

The wooden hull should be checked for the presence of dry rot. "Dry rot" is a misnomer since dry wood does not rot. The organisms that cause the rot exist only if the wood is saturated with moisture. Rot can occur during the off-season when moisture condenses on the inside of the hull and rainwater wets the outside. The most likely places for rot to appear are around the transom and behind the moldings. Before caulking and painting a wood hull, replace any planks showing evidence of rot. One method of preventing rot is to apply a liberal coat of linseed oil. The oil does not allow moisture to collect.

It is a good practice to repaint a wood or plywood hull before the beginning of each season. First scrub and then sand the hull thoroughly if the surface is in good shape. Spot paint any bare spots and replace any caulking that is holding badly or appears powdery. Next apply a fresh coat of marine-grade paint. All work on the boat should be done in a sheltered area. Neither paint nor caulking will adhere very well if the wood contains the slightest amount of moisture.

After a time it is best that a wood hull be entirely refinished, instead of applying coat upon coat of paint. Apply a few coats of paint remover to the hull and, when the paint lifts, remove it with a putty knife. Next the hull should be scraped with a triangular-bladed boat scraper. Sand the hull to smooth it out and remove all traces of the old paint. Before caulking apply a coat of primer. This will allow the filler to get a better hold on the wood. Apply two coats of marine-grade paint, sanding lightly after the first, and the job is complete.

Compared to a wooden hull, a hull made of aluminum requires

little maintenance. A soap or mild detergent and a soft scrub brush can be used to clean the hull. To preserve the metallic finish, the hull may be waxed using any one of a number of products. Also, a clear lacquer can be applied.

Aluminum forms a protective layer of oxide film which prevents corrosion. Because of this, there is no real need to paint an aluminum hull. When corrosion does occur, small grayish patches of powder appear, but they in no way harm the hull or affect its efficiency.

The only reason to paint an aluminum hull is esthetics. Boat owners find the aluminum glaring and like a colorful boat. To paint an aluminum hull first clean and rinse it thoroughly. Next apply a phosphoric acid solution, which will increase the adhesion of the paint, and rinse with fresh water. Before applying the final paint, two grades of primer may be needed. One grade can be applied to ordinary surfaces and the second, antifouling primer, is used on the bottom. The antifouling primer helps to keep algae and barnacles off the bottom of the boat.

Dents and scratches on aluminum hulls can be repaired by using a metallic putty. For use on colored hulls, a matching putty can be purchased. The best method for repairing a hull is a double patch. The first step is to cut out a hole larger than the puncture and shape a patch so that it fits exactly into the hole. Rivet a larger patch to the inside of the boat. Then attach the smaller patch from the outside to the larger patch. Use caulking to seal around the patches.

Regular cleaning and waxing of a fibreglass hull will help lessen the effects of dirt. Under the influence of dirt, the original finish can fade and the smooth surface break down. The thickness of the hull's surface finish or gel may, however, fade away. Also, the surface can become scratched and gouged. Spot painting and the use of a matching filler may not be enough, and the hull will have to be refinished.

To refinish a fiberglass hull, the surface wax must first be removed by using a wax solvent and then the gel coating eliminated. It is very difficult to refinish fiberglass without removing the gel, because it provides a poor adhesive surface for the paint. The gel must be sanded off, rendering the hull rough before painting. Antifouling paint should be applied to the bottom, and it is a good idea to repaint the bottom every year.

Engine Maintenance

The basic procedures for readying outboards, inboards, and sterndrives are about the same. The engine manual, which lists maintenance details and specifications, is invaluable. If it is lost, contact the manufacturer and he will generally supply a new one free of charge. A yard mechanic can be commissioned to prepare the engine, but it is not a difficult process should you want to do it yourself.

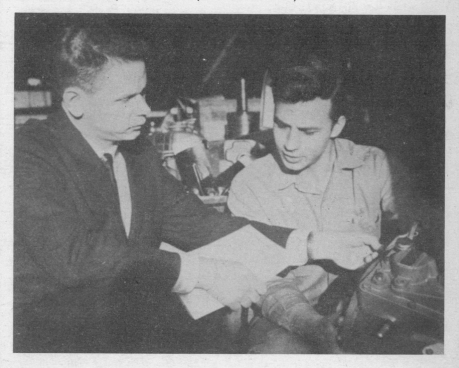

Doing Engine Maintenance

New, properly gapped spark plugs should be installed. The manual will list the plug type and gap setting. The carburetor float bowl should be cleaned. While afloat, the carburetor can be tuned by adjusting knobs marked "high speed" and "low speed" or by turning the idle screw. Working with a warm engine, turn the "high speed" knob until the motor sounds as if it is running smoothly. The "low speed" knob and the idle screw are adjusted with the engine idling. Turn until the motor seems about to stall, then turn slowly in the opposite direction until the motor runs smoothly and quietly.

Inspect the cooling system hoses and replace any that seem even the slightest bit worn or cracked. A broken or leaky hose can overheat the motor and, if the leak goes unchecked, can flood the bilge.

Check the manual to see which parts need lubrication. On outboards, the lower unit will need a lubrication change. Remove the two screw plugs on the drive section of the motor and allow the old lubrication to seep out before putting in the new. In addition, a light coat of oil should be placed around the motor clamp screws and the throttle linkage. On inboards and sterndrives, change and replace the crankcase oil and the oil filter cartridge. A small amount of oil or grease should be placed in the cups located near the water pump, distributor, and generator.

If the motor is equipped with an electric starter, check the battery charge and, if necessary, fill up the cells with distilled water. Inspect the terminals for corrosion and clean them with diluted ammonia. Examine the ignition wiring and replace any that is even slightly cracked.

To prevent corrosion of the outer engine housing, wipe it with an oily rag. Retouch any rusty spots or places where the paint is peeling. And, finally, tighten the engine mounting bolts.

DURING THE SEASON

After each run, hose down the boat with fresh water. This will prevent salt water from corroding the upper hull. Once in a while use mild soap. Touch up any spots that appear worn.

Maintenance will vary from engine to engine and the manual is the best guide. But usually the crankcase oil should be replaced after every 100 hours of use, the gearbox oil changed after every 50 hours, and the spark plugs checked after every 25. If necessary, clean and regap the plugs. If the spark plug gaps are too small, they will continually foul and rob the engine of power. If the gaps are too large, the engine will be difficult to start.

To prevent cluttering, remove any gear that is no longer of use.

Boats in Winter Storage

WINTER

There are three storage choices for a boat during the winter months. Indoor garage storage is probably the most advantageous, but few people are blessed with a garage large enough to house their boat. The boat must be properly suspended, because without sufficient support the hull can become distorted. Wooden shelving or placement on horses are equal to the task. Never store a wooden boat in a heated garage. The wood will dry, opening the seams.

Most boats are stored outdoors under a protective canopy, usually made of canvas. Rig a series of A-frames and a ridgepole. The A-frames can be notched so they fit tightly against the gunwales. Run a line through the grommets and attach it at intervals to the trailer or cradle. To allow ventilation, slit the cover in a few places and then loosely stitch the edges together.

Securing the boat to a slip and then leaving it for the winter is called wet storage. Moor the boat in an ice-free location, as the pressure of ice can split the hull. Since the boat is to remain afloat for the winter, it is a good idea to paint the bottom before storage, protecting the hull from barnacles and shipworms.

Before putting the boat in storage, open all doors and hatches to ventilate the boat, remove all excess gear to help prevent the boat from distorting under the extra weight, and drain the head with disinfectant.

Winterizing the Motor

The first step in winterizing the motor is to drain all fuel and water. Allow the motor to run with the fuel line disconnected. This will burn up any gasoline left in the carburetor. Empty the fuel tanks and examine them for dirt and rust. If they are present, flush the tanks with kerosene. Water in the tanks can be removed with commercial alcohol. If the cooling system uses salt water, run fresh water into it to wash away any salt deposits. To eject any remaining water, manually turn the starter a few times. To a fresh-water cooled engine add antifreeze.

Remove the sparkplugs, inject a corrosion-inhibitor into the holes, and put the plugs back. For inboards and sterndrives, change the crankcase oil. The internal parts should be coated with oil. Take the top cover off the outboard and spray light oil on all the moving parts. Oil fed into the carburetor on an inboard or sterndrive will distribute the oil over all the moving parts.

Clean corrosion from the battery terminals by using distilled ammonia. If necessary, fill the cells with distilled water. The battery should be stored in a dry place not subject to temperature fluctuations. Remove the propeller and clean the shaft with sandpaper or steel wool and apply grease. Replace the propeller.

Chapter 14
Berthing The Boat

Locating a berth for the boat is becoming increasingly difficult as the number of boats soars. Most people are not fortunate enough to own a piece of the waterfront, and must choose from among five alternatives: a yacht club, a marina, a boatyard, an offshore mooring, or a trailer.

For the price of the fee, from $5 a year to more than $1000, the typical yacht club offers in addition to a mooring or slip, various social privileges including dinners, dances, a club restaurant, and organized racing. Most yacht clubs have a long waiting list.

Marinas, for a nominal cost, provide some of the same services as yacht clubs and offer both slip and mooring berths. A slip is a wooden stall either perpendicular (a pier) or parallel (a wharf) to the shore. A mooring is an offshore anchorage point, usually a float or a buoy, to which a boat line is attached. Slips are more expensive than moorings because they are more convenient. Loading and unloading, hosing down the boat, and generally coming and going at will are some of the advantages of a slip. To reach a boat at mooring requires ferrying on a dinghy, usually provided by the marina. Loading a boat from a dinghy can be risky. Slip costs are based on overall boat lengths in feet, ranging from $3 to more than $15 per foot. A new development is dry-land marinas for outboards. The boats are stored on racks and lifted out for use by a fork lift. Usual marina facilities include winter storage, fuel, maintenance and repair, a supply store, watchmen, and a restaurant.

If a boatyard is used for winter storage, it is quite possible that the yard will rent slip or mooring space. Boatyard berthing is less expensive than a marina slip. However, the services are limited, though the usual facilities include bathrooms, and rowboats to reach the mooring.

An offshore mooring can be rented for as little as $5 for the season. Care must be taken in choosing the site. The ideal place should be free from waves, tidal flows, and stream channels. In addition, it should be sheltered from wind. Provision has to be made for storing the rowboat or dinghy both on and offshore.

Except for the initial expense of its purchase, a trailer used as a dry-land berthing costs nothing. Storage of gear at home avoids the problems of vandalism, theft, and damage due to weather. The best way to launch a boat from a trailer is to use a graded ramp. The ramp should be covered with cement, asphalt, or crushed rock. Never attempt to launch from a sandy beach, as the car may sink into the sand.

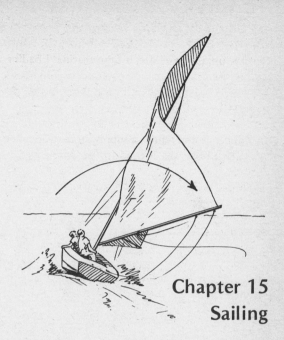

Chapter 15
Sailing

Sailing has its own particular kind of pleasure. More than motorboating, sailing requires learned skills. The mystique of sailing is in no small way due to the correct use of the oldest power available: the wind. A man's taming of the wind, putting it to work for his own pleasure and sport, is both a victory of spirit and a compliment to nature.

TYPES OF SAILBOATS

The Racing Sailboat

Most of the racing sailboats under 24 feet have a centerboard, rather than a keel. The hull can be constructed of plywood or fiberglass, and its possible shape includes flat, round, and V-bottoms. The racing sailboat can be transported by trailer and launched directly from the beach. The hulls are shallow enough to permit sailing in shoal waters.

Racing sailboats are broken down into one-design classes. Though these may be built by different manufacturers, the same plans and specifications are used. Within a class, the contest is one of seamanship and skill rather than the better boat.

There are many, many different one-design classes. The following is only a partial listing of the most popular.

Blue Jay: Measuring only 13½ feet, the Blue Jay is used primarily as a junior trainer. The jib and mainsail area is 90 square feet without a spinnaker. The hull is made of sheet plywood.

Snipe

    Snipe: The Snipe is the largest and oldest one-design class. The 15½-foot V-bottom hull can have plywood, plank, or fiberglass construction. The total sail area is 108 square feet, and it is a fast and sensitive boat.

Rebel: A favorite in the Midwest, this 16-footer has a fiberglass hull.

Hampton: This sloop can float in about 8 inches of water and is popular around Chesapeake Bay. She is 18 feet long.

Jet 14: Being a planing-hull boat, the Jet 14 is capable of very fast speeds. It is an extremely light, two-man boat. The total sail area is 113 square feet.

Lightning

Lightning: The Lightning is popular as a family boat. Its 19-foot length supports a roomy cockpit and is easy to handle. It has 177 square feet of sail area and a planked hull.

International 14: This is a fast 14-foot sloop. The planing hull is constructed of molded fiberglass or plywood.

Star

Star: One of the oldest one-design classes, the Star is strictly a two-man racing boat. Its planked hull measures 23 feet.

Thistle: The Thistle can be used for both racing and family sailing. The boat is 17 feet long and the hull is made of molded plywood.

5-O-5: This sloop is definitely not for beginners. It is extremely fast and makes for a thrilling ride. This 16-footer has a planing hull of molded plywood.

Cruising Sailboat

The Cruising Sailboat

The majority of cruising sailboats are fitted with either outboard or inboard power as well as sails. The hull is usually made of fiberglass and has built-in flotation. Cabin accommodations can include two berths, a head, and a small galley with a stove. Cruising sailboats are 24 feet and under, and most can be transported by trailer.

Like racing sailboats, cruising sailboats have one-design classes. The most popular include the Marauder, a 16-footer good for weekend traveling; the Bear, a 23-footer designed for rough water and winds, with a wooden hull; and the Corsaire, with a good size cabin built into its 18-foot length.

PARTS OF THE SAILBOAT

The Rigging

The rigging is the system of ropes and wires that support the mast (standing rigging) and control the movement of the sails (running rigging).

The standing rigging consists of wires called the shrouds and stays. Shrouds support the mast against sideways motion; stays hold the mast in relation to fore-and-aft. Depending on the height of the mast, there can be an upper and lower shroud. It is important to have the shrouds taut, but not too tight or too loose. Both upper and lower shrouds should be equally taut. The stays include the jibstay or headstay, jumper stays, and a permanent backstay. As the wind blows against the sails, the mainsail pushes the mast aft and the jib pulls it forward. To balance these forces, the jumper stays, which are attached to the masthead over the jumper strut, offset the forward pulling jibstays. However, the mast as a whole is still being pulled forward by the jib, and the permanent backstay, attached to the masthead and transom, counteracts this force.

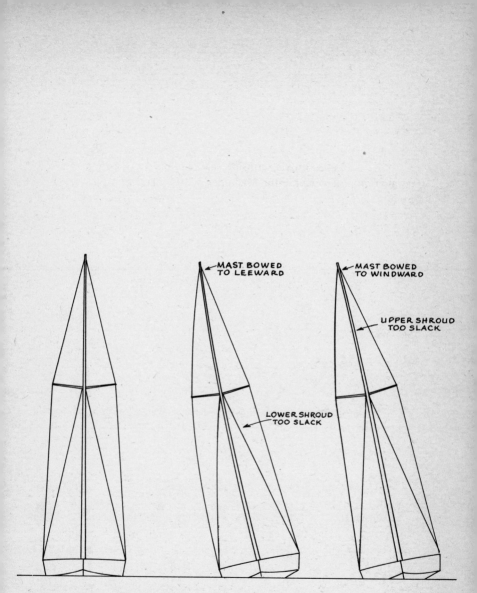

MAST BOWED
TO LEEWARD

MAST BOWED
TO WINDWARD

UPPER SHROUD
TOO SLACK

LOWER SHROUD
TOO SLACK

Diagram of Standard Rigging

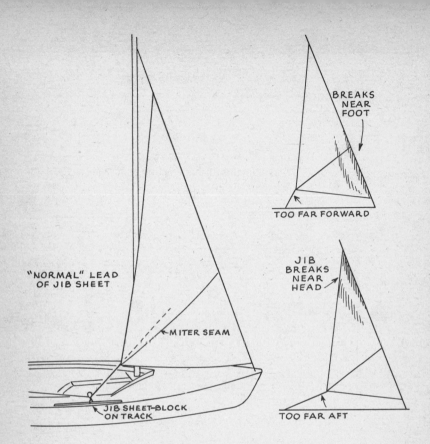

BREAKS
NEAR
FOOT

TOO FAR FORWARD

"NORMAL" LEAD
OF JIB SHEET

JIB
BREAKS
NEAR
HEAD

MITER SEAM

JIB SHEET-BLOCK
ON TRACK

TOO FAR AFT

Diagram of Running Rigging

The running rigging includes halyards, sheets, and guys. The halyards are used to raise the sails. They run up and over the mast, and back down to the deck. Each sail has its own halyard. Sheets are used to turn the sails. The main sheet is attached to the boom and runs through a series of pulleys, called blocks. The purpose of the blocks is to relieve the force of the main sheet exerted by the mainsail. There are two jib sheets, only one of which is taut at a particular time. They control the angle of the jib. The guys are used to control the spinnaker.

146

The Sails

Small sailboats have three types of sails: the mainsail, the jib, and the spinnaker. Most sails are made of dacron. Unlike cotton sails, dacron sails will not mildew or rot, shrink when wet, or stretch.

The mainsail is secured to the mast at three places: the head, the tack, and the clew. The head is attached to the main halyard and is the top of the sail. The tack attaches boom to mast. The clew is at the bottom of the sail. The ideal mainsail shape is like an airfoil. Battens are flat wood or plastic strips that fit into the mainsail and help preserve its shape.

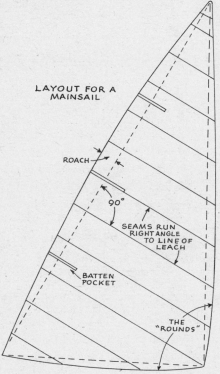

LAYOUT FOR A
MAINSAIL

ROACH

90°

SEAMS RUN
RIGHT ANGLE
TO LINE OF
LEACH

BATTEN
POCKET

THE
"ROUNDS"

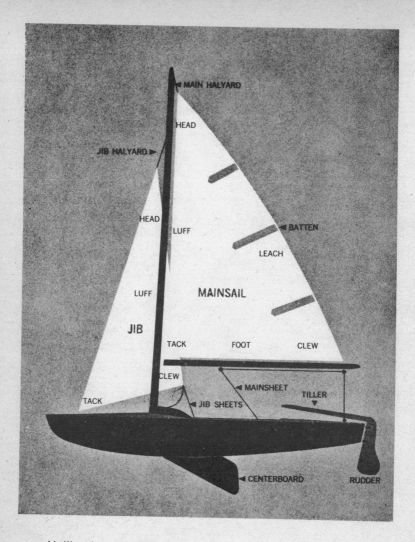

Unlike the rounded mainsail, the jib is usually cut triangular. It is raised forward of the mainsail, and its purpose is to funnel wind into the mainsail.

U.S. Department of Commerce, Weather Bureau

Cirrus clouds are the first indication of an approaching warm front.

U.S. Department of Commerce, Weather Bureau

An indication of the second stage of a warm front is the appearance of cirro-stratus clouds.

The appearance of cumulus clouds often signals the build-up of thunderstorms.

U.S. Department of Commerce, Weather Bureau

An anvil-shaped cloud warns of the approach of a violent thunderstorm.

A mackerel sky (banded altocumulus clouds) warns of the approach of a cold front and possible rain.

U.S. Department of Commerce, Weather Bureau

Fractocumulus clouds indicate the approach of clearing, colder weather.

Stratocumulus clouds of early morning break up and become fair-weather cumulus clouds as the sun rises.

1.
DETACH SPINNAKER
POLE FROM MAST

2.
SNAP POLE TO
OTHER CORNER
OF SAIL

3.
AS MAINSAIL JIBES,
RELEASE POLE FROM
OLD CORNER

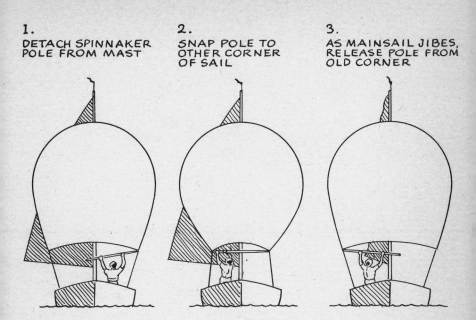

The spinnaker is a large nylon sail shaped somewhat like a parachute. It is designed to catch even the lightest of breezes and, because it can move at right angles to the wind, the spinnaker greatly increases the boat's speed.

FUNDAMENTALS OF SAILING

The sail acts as an airfoil, similar to an airplane wing. As the wind passes around the sail, a vacuum is created at the rear driving the boat forward. The centerboard or keel prevents the boat from sliding sideways.

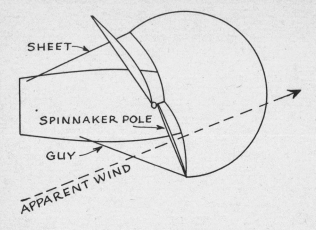

SHEET

SPINNAKER POLE

GUY

APPARENT WIND

"Two" winds must be considered while sailing: the true wind and the apparent wind. The sails should be trimmed in relation to the apparent wind, which is actually the stronger. This phenomenon is called in physics the parallelogram of forces. In sailing, it is known as sailing to windward.

A boat cannot sail directly into the wind. The best angle that can be achieved is 45 degrees off the true wind direction. There are three basic sailing positions: sailing into the wind at 45 degrees (beating), sailing with the wind coming directly from astern (running), and sailing at right angles to the wind (reaching).

Beating

In beating, the sails are trimmed in close. In order to sail in a windward direction, a series of maneuvers, called tacking, is required. The boat travels first to one side of the wind, comes about, and then travels on the other side.

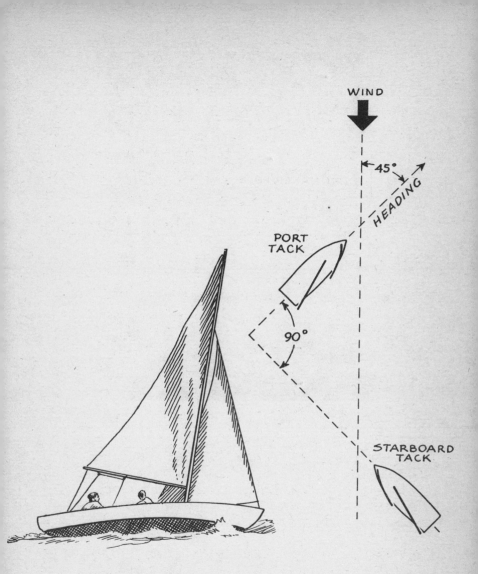

Sailboat Beating

Sailing at an angle less than 45 degrees results in luffing, or sail flutter, which distorts the ideal airfoil shape. The common method of getting the right amount of trim is to loosen both the mainsail and the jib until the luff appears and then tighten the sails until it vanishes. Sailing too far off the wind, at an angle greater than 45 degrees, results in sluggish performance.

Since turns are a necessary part of tacking, it is important to know how a sailboat is steered. If the tiller, which is attached to the rudder, is turned toward the left, or port, the boat will travel to the right, or starboard.

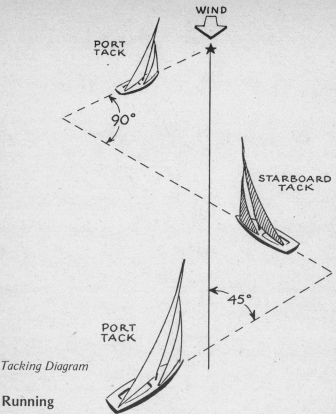

WIND

PORT
TACK

90°

STARBOARD
TACK

45°

PORT
TACK

Tacking Diagram

Running

Running, or sailing in the same direction as the wind, is usually easy sailing. The mainsail and spinnaker are let out and the boat theoretically can travel at the same speed as the wind, limited only by the water friction on the hull.

Running in a strong wind requires a great deal of vigilance on the part of the helmsman. He must watch out for waves coming up from astern, which can swing the stern around. Using the rudder, the helmsman can make corrections for the action of the waves and keep the boat heading downwind.

WIND

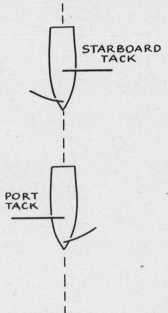

STARBOARD
TACK

PORT
TACK

Running

When running, never sail with the wind leeward. The result can be an accidental jibbing as the mainsail and boom swing about across the cockpit. Capsizing is very likely to occur. Always be aware of the wind direction. It is never constant and shifts as great as 20 degrees can happen. Corrective action must be taken immediately with the helm to swing the boat with the changing wind.

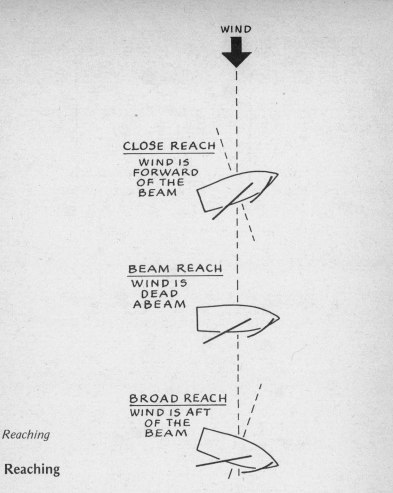

WIND

CLOSE REACH
WIND IS
FORWARD
OF THE
BEAM

BEAM REACH
WIND IS
DEAD
ABEAM

BROAD REACH
WIND IS AFT
OF THE
BEAM

Reaching

Reaching

Reaching is sailing at a course about 90 degrees to the wind. It is the simplest and the fastest of the sailing positions. Any point between beating and running is reaching. A close reach occurs when the course is less than 90 degrees to the wind. A far reach is more than 90 degrees.

In reaching, the sails are trimmed in the same manner as in beating. They are let out until a luff appears and then trimmed until it vanishes.

159

WHAT IS IT?

Sailboat Rigs

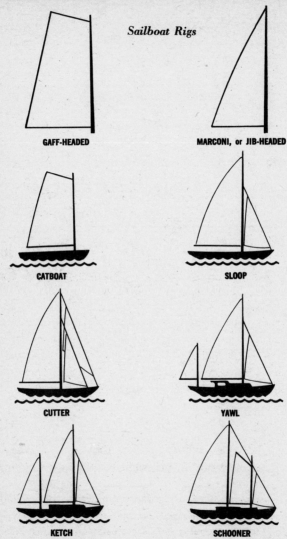

GAFF-HEADED

MARCONI, or JIB-HEADED

CATBOAT

SLOOP

CUTTER

YAWL

KETCH

SCHOONER

Chapter 16
Specialized Craft

INFLATABLES

Fabric-hull inflatables are extremely light craft that will stay afloat even if most of the air compartments are deflated. They squat on the surface and, if adequately powered and lightly loaded, inflatables can achieve a high speed with a small outboard.

WATER SCOOTERS

Water scooters are marine motorcycles. They have handlebars which control the throttle. Water scooters are mainly short-haul, fun boats, and can be fitted with enough power to carry two passengers and pull two skiers.

Inflatable

Water Scooter

Collapsible

COLLAPSIBLES

Collapsible boats can be unfolded and seaworthy in only a few minutes. The boat is light enough to be carried to the water before assembly. A collapsible takes a small outboard and is economical in both initial cost and running.

CANOES

A canoe is a light, narrow boat usually moved with paddles. However, there are now powered canoes on the market. A side bracket for the outboard is eliminated on many models by a square stern.

Amphibian

AMPHIBIANS

An amphibian can travel on both land and water. Most amphibians are more suited for land and swamp use than for cruising. Much of the power is wasted as an amphibian travels through water and they are extremely slow, traveling about 4 MPH.

AIRBOATS

Airboats are propelled along the surface by a large fan mounted at the stern. They can operate over water, swamp lands, sand, and snow. A model equipped with 180 hp can reach a speed of 60 MPH.

Airboat

HOVERCRAFT

Hovercraft travel about four inches above the surface on a cushion of air. Over flat land and calm water, they can reach speeds of up to 40 MPH. When the down-thrust engine is turned off, the boat acts as a displacement hull.

ACKNOWLEDGMENTS

JOHNSON MOTORS:

Pages 10, 46, 80, 162

MOBIL OIL:

Page 64

STRIKER:

Pages 16, 17

OLD TOWN CANOE:

Page 165

PENN YAN:

Pages 40, 41

U.S. COAST GUARD:

Pages 57, 60, 113

GLASTRON:

Pages 43, 50

BOY SCOUTS OF AMERICA:

Pages 54, 121, 123

LUGER:

Page 48